Crown Financial Ministries

COMPANION
GUIDE

D1213495

ISBN 978-1-56427-333-8

Portions originally published under the titles:

Using Your Money Wisely by Larry Burkett (Moody Press Trade, 1990).

God is Faithful by Larry Burkett and Chuck Bentley (Crown Financial Minstries, 2013).

MoneyLife® Personal Finance Study by Crown Financial Ministries (Crown Financial Ministries, 2013).

Portions of this book were taken from content previously published in other Crown Financial Ministries materials.

Printed in the United States of America

Crown MoneyLife
personal finance study

Overcoming Financial Challenges To Help You Achieve a Life of Meaning and Purpose

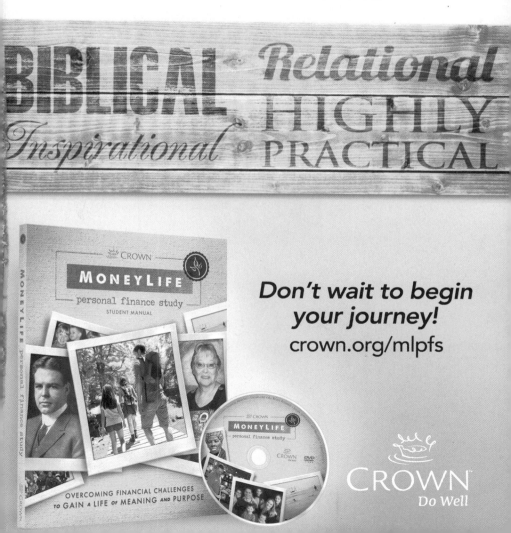

BIBLICAL *Relational*
Inspirational HIGHLY PRACTICAL

Don't wait to begin your journey!
crown.org/mlpfs

CROWN
Do Well

Crown
OutReach
P A R T N E R S™

You're invited to help transform our world...

Consider the way God moved in your life.. Anything God has done for you through Crown was made possible by someone investing in this ministry.

Now you're invited to lead the way in sharing with others... as a Crown Outreach Partner.

Visit us online or call to find out more and discover the membership benefit package available to Outreach Partners.

crown.org/outreachpartners or 800-722-1976.

Mark 11:15-17
Luke 19:45-46
John 2:14-16
2 Corinthians 12:14
1 Timothy 3:2-3
1 Timothy 3:8
1 Timothy 6:5-6
Titus 1:10-11
1 Peter 5:1-2
Ecclesiastes 5:10-11
Song of Solomon 8:7
Isaiah 24:2
Isaiah 52:3
Lamentations 4:1-2
Matthew 22:5
Luke 12:13-15
Luke 16:1-14
Acts 8:18-24
1 Corinthians 10:33

2 Corinthians 6:4, 10
Colossians 3:1-5
1 Timothy 4:4
Hebrews 10:34
Hebrews 11:24-26
1 John 2:15-17
2 Samuel 18:11-12
1 Kings 15:16-20
2 Kings 16:5, 8-9
2 Chronicles 16:2-4
Isaiah 59:2, 4
Matthew 5:25-26
Matthew 5:40
Luke 6:29-30
Luke 12:58-59
1 Corinthians 6:1-8
Acts 16:16-19
Acts 19:24-27

For a full listing and explanation of scriptures please visit
crown.org/scripture.

Acknowledgements

Chuck Bentley

Years ago, you recognized the need to create the original Crown Money Map, a pathway to true financial freedom which has now been followed by millions of people. Thank you for your dedication to seeking God's vision for the Money Map, and for your commitment to improving it ever since. The Lord has used you and the Money Map to transform a great many of his children. Thank you for shaping the purpose of this guide.

Hannah Simic, Steve Brooks, Susan Ellington, Sheila Thompson

Thank you for your vision and belief that this guide would be a great tool to help those on the Money Map journey. Thank you for the many hours spent researching and providing insight into the contents. Your knowledge and desire to help hurting people is what fuels this book. I pray that you will see God change lives through this guide, and hear the testimonies of those who have been blessed by it.

Katie Logan, Arielle Vogel

Your keen eyes and intuition helped in crafting the shape and content of this book. Thank you for keeping the melody of this book consistent, beautiful, and meaningful.

Robert Dickie III, Heather Stanfield, Handre De Jongh, Susan Ellington, Kim Cooper, Katie Logan, Hannah Simic, Sheila Thompson

Thank you for your hard work to create the updated Money Map. Your collected wisdom, creativity, and insight provided a roadmap that sparked the creation of this book. Without your input and prayers, this book would never have been written and published. May you be elated in how God chooses to use this book.

Jim Alexander, Jim Armstrong, Sean Allen, Dwayne Bassett

Your wisdom and technical knowledge is astounding and a gift from God. Thank you for your professionalism and expertise in helping us to put this work into the hands of those who need it. I pray that God will use you to aid many other writers and projects, all to His glory!

TABLE OF CONTENTS

———

Introduction

Welcome to the *Crown Money Map® Companion Guide*. By now, you have your Crown Money Map® in hand and have probably familiarized yourself with the various destinations. So how are you feeling? Excited and motivated, or confused and overwhelmed? Regardless of where you find yourself, my hope is that this Companion Guide will serve as a reference and encouragement for you along your journey.

Throughout the pages that follow, you will hear testimonies of others who have faced similar circumstances. You will have the chance to dig into Scripture, keep a journal, set goals, and learn more about God's principles for becoming His faithful steward as you make progress towards your goal of true financial freedom. You will also find practical tips and resource recommendations for each destination.

This Companion Guide is organized by destination. Keep the book nearby, and after you have celebrated completing a destination, grab this guide and recharge for your next destination. Or, if you find yourself stuck or discouraged in the middle of a destination, spend some time reading through testimonies, studying the scriptures listed in the back, or journaling your specific prayers to God. Most of all, our hope and prayer is that the Lord will give you hope, determination, and encouragement to complete this journey and your financial goals.

The financial principles given throughout God's Word are not there to see if we're strong enough to live by them—they're given because God knows that they are the best for us. God's principles of finances are not an arbitrary set of rules by which to govern us—they are a loving Father's wisdom to those who will listen and trust Him.

It surprises many Christians to learn that approximately two-thirds of the parables that Christ used in His teaching deal specifically with finances. The reason for that is very simple— He chose a topic with which everyone could identify. A parable is a form of teaching using story to magnify a spiritual truth. Christ was describing a spiritual kingdom that is actually more real than this material kingdom, so in order to communicate it, He often used a common worldly tool—money.

Christ never said money or material things were evil. He said that they are often symptoms of the real root problems. He constantly warned us to guard our hearts against greed, covetousness, ego, and pride, because those are the tools that Satan uses to control and manipulate this world. Christ warned us a great deal about the sin of materialism.

"And He said to them, 'Beware, and be on your guard against every form of greed; for not even when one has an abundance does his life consist of his possessions'"
Luke 12:15 NASB

In fact, in the parable about salvation in Matthew 13:18-23, "the deceitfulness of riches" is given as a cause for unfruitfulness.

Satan desires to take the very riches provided by God to enhance our lives and bring others to salvation and cause us to become greedy and use them only on our own selfish needs and pleasures.

Your journey to true financial freedom

So what is *true financial freedom* and how do you know when you've arrived? Is it just a final destination or is it more like a journey? Based on the title of this Companion Guide, you know we believe it is a journey. It is possible to be completely debt free, tithing, saving—even wealthy—and not experience the true financial freedom God intends for His people. On the other hand, it is also possible to experience true financial freedom very early in your journey. True financial freedom is based largely on the condition of our heart and attitude, not just the condition of our finances.

Let's look at an example in Scripture. In Mark 10:

> [17] *As Jesus started on his way, a man ran up to him and fell on his knees before him. "Good teacher," he asked, "what must I do to inherit eternal life?"*
>
> [18] *"Why do you call me good?" Jesus answered. "No one is*

good—except God alone.¹⁹ You know the commandments: 'You shall not murder, you shall not commit adultery, you shall not steal, you shall not give false testimony, you shall not defraud, honor your father and mother.'"

²⁰ "Teacher," he declared, "all these I have kept since I was a boy."

²¹ Jesus looked at him and loved him. "One thing you lack," he said. "Go, sell everything you have and give to the poor, and you will have treasure in heaven. Then come, follow me."

²² At this the man's face fell. He went away sad, because he had great wealth.

²³ Jesus looked around and said to his disciples, "How hard it is for the rich to enter the kingdom of God!"

²⁴ The disciples were amazed at his words. But Jesus said again, "Children, how hard it is to enter the kingdom of God! ²⁵ It is easier for a camel to go through the eye of a needle than for someone who is rich to enter the kingdom of God."

²⁶ The disciples were even more amazed, and said to each other, "Who then can be saved?"

²⁷ Jesus looked at them and said, "With man this is impossible, but not with God; all things are possible with God."

²⁸ Then Peter spoke up, "We have left everything to follow you!"

²⁹ *"Truly I tell you," Jesus replied, "no one who has left home or brothers or sisters or mother or father or children or fields for me and the gospel* ³⁰ *will fail to receive a hundred times as much in this present age: homes, brothers, sisters, mothers, children and fields— along with persecutions—and in the age to come eternal life.* ³¹ *But many who are first will be last, and the last first"*

NIV

This rich young ruler was financially independent. We can probably assume he had no debt, plenty of savings in the bank and no financial worries. However, as the story continues, we see that he was not truly financially free in Christ. His response to Jesus reveals he was living in bondage to his wealth. It was more important for him to keep his money than to receive the true riches Jesus was offering him.

The majority of warnings in Christ's messages were addressed to the rich, those whose hearts were dependent upon money for their identity and security. Among the wealthy, anxieties and worries are not related to the lack of things but rather to the loss of things. Many people fear the loss of the material goods they have acquired. Therefore, they compromise God's best for their lives to hang on to what they fear they will lose, just as the rich young ruler did. Surrendering to the Lord does not necessarily mean surrendering the assets. It means placing our complete identity and security in Christ.

Just a couple of chapters later in Mark 12 we meet a poor widow.

> [41] *Jesus sat down opposite the place where the offerings were put and watched the crowd putting their money into the temple treasury. Many rich people threw in large amounts.* [42] *But a poor widow came and put in two very small copper coins, worth only a few cents.*
>
> [43] *Calling his disciples to him, Jesus said, "Truly I tell you, this poor widow has put more into the treasury than all the others.* [44] *They all gave out of their wealth; but she, out of her poverty, put in everything—all she had to live on".*
>
> NIV

This widow, declared poor by Jesus himself, gave out of her poverty. She demonstrated true financial freedom in her willingness to respond to God's call on her life. She expressed absolute trust in God to provide for her needs. She had no back up plan. She is known for all time as an example of extreme trust in Christ, for which she was commended.

When compared to the rich young ruler, the widow had much more financial freedom. She also demonstrated her contentment was not dependent on her bank account.

Crown's founder, Larry Burkett, defined contentment as knowing God's plan for your life, having the conviction to live it, and believing that God's peace is greater than the world's problems.

Often we get so involved in the day-to-day activities of earning a living and raising a family that we forget our real purpose: to serve God. Consequently trivial problems such as buying a new car or attaining a higher position begin to crowd our hearts, and God's plan is no longer our priority or focus.

God wants us to understand that money is a tool to use in accomplishing His plan through us. He wants us to be living stewards of everything He entrusts to us: our time, talents, and resources. But, this requires contentment. If we are to find true contentment, we must establish some basic guidelines:

8 guidelines for finding true contentment

1. Establish a reasonable standard of living.
2. Establish a habit of giving.
3. Establish priorities.
4. Develop a thankful attitude.
5. Reject a fearful spirit.
6. Seek God's will for your life.
7. Stand up to the fear.
8. Trust God's promises.

Next step

On the back of your Money Map, you will see a declaration of your role as a steward—one entrusted with the property of God. These five statements are intended to keep you focused on placing your trust in God, finding contentment, and ultimately becoming His good and faithful steward. Say these aloud, even now:

God owns it all.
God's way is always better than my way, so I give Him control.
I am content with what God has provided.
I am God's wise manager.
I am free to fulfill God's plans for my life and advance His kingdom.

In the days ahead, I hope you'll return to these truths and hide them in your heart. Look up and memorize the verses that go with each. Allow the principles to become rooted deep within your heart.

As you begin your journey, I want to remind you of Paul's words in Philippians 4:11b-12 (NIV): "*I have learned to be content whatever the circumstances. I know what it is to be in need, and I know what it is to have plenty. I have learned the secret of being content in any and every situation, whether well fed or hungry, whether living in plenty or in want.*" Paul claims he's learned the secret of being content in any and every situation. So what is it? In verse 13 he goes on to reveal his secret: "*I can do all this through him who gives me strength.*"

Now, commit your journey to the Lord and always depend upon Him, especially when you become discouraged along the way.

We recommend that you use the Destinations in the Money Map to begin your journey one step at a time. While you may have partially completed a number of different steps within each Destination, it is best to fully complete the requirements of each one. For instance, if you have not begun to give God the first portion of your income or you have yet to save $1,000, accomplishing these steps will give you great joy and encouragement to make the next steps.

As you begin, remember we are here to serve you. Feel free to reach out to us at any time to assist you. Now, may God give you the desires of your heart according to His promise in Psalm 37:4.

DESTINATION 1:

BUILD EMERGENCY SAVINGS

The wise man saves for the future, but the foolish man spends whatever he gets.

PROVERBS 21:20 TLB

In This Destination...

1. Track spending and create your spending plan

2. Save $1,000 for emergencies

3. Start giving regularly to the Lord

DATE COMPLETED: _____

What is true contentment?

By freeing yourself from your financial burdens, you become more capable of serving the Lord and being a faithful steward of His resources. This will bring you contentment. As we discussed in the introduction, contentment, contrary to popular opinion, is not being satisfied where you are. It is knowing God's plan for your life, having the conviction to live it, and believing that God's peace is greater than the world's problems.

God wants us to be savers. He wants us to save and have extra resources to take care of our families and be in a position to serve Him and others so that He will be made known and honored. His Word also warns that saving to become self-reliant and just to take life easy is wrong. Balancing your savings is an opportunity to honor God and experience His blessings.

"For which of you, desiring to build a tower, does not first sit down and count the cost, whether he has enough to complete it? Otherwise, when he has laid a foundation and is not able to finish, all who see it begin to mock him, saying, 'This man began to build and was not able to finish.'"

(Luke 14:28-30 ESV)

Though Jesus was talking about the cost of following Him, this illustration can also be applied to our finances. No one starts out in life planning to struggle from paycheck to paycheck or to live with an overwhelming burden of debt. However, if we don't make a plan for dealing with the unexpected, we can end up like the man in Jesus' story—staring up at a half-built tower of financial chaos, without the means or the strategy in place to make things right.

As we better understand what God's Word says about managing our resources, we may realize additional areas that need improvement. We can always change. If we truly desire to be to be a good steward, we must align our hearts with God and pursue the right motive for doing those things. The end result is that God will be honored and made known to a needy world.

PRACTICAL TOOLS

Track spending and create your spending plan

If you do not already have a budget, creating one can be freeing! It can bring you peace and break the bonds of being a slave to money.

Start off by determining your income. From this point on, accurately track your spending. Is this the first time you have written out where all your money goes? If so, it can seem daunting to create an initial budget, because you may not even know exactly how much you need in each category. If you have bank records or keep old receipts, do your best to get an accurate view of how much you typically spend in a month and what you spend it on. This will help you to know how much to put into each category in your spending plan.

HINT: Many people carry a small notepad or use their mobile phone to record all their expenditures. Be sure to note the category of each expenditure.

List all of your regular bills and debts. Even write out what day of the month they are due, their normal amount, and how often are they paid (ex: monthly, quarterly, etc.).

You will also need to look at your recent pay stubs to determine your withholdings.

Now with all of this knowledge, you can create your spending plan. We recommend using either the interactive, online MoneyLife® Planner or one of our printable budget forms.

MoneyLife® Budget Planner	Crown Financial Statements
• Online	• Printable
• Interactive	• Fill out with a computer or
• Tracks your income and	by hand
spending	• Creates graphs from data
https://planner.crown.org	www.crown.org/printbudget

After you have been on your plan for a month, compare your spending plan to the guideline budget on page 25. Can you make adjustments in your spending plan to align more with the guideline budget (you don't have be in exact alignment)? Once you have an accurate view of your spending, you can adjust it to make sure it matches your "net spendable income."

Save $1,000 for emergencies

The first step is to open a savings account at your local bank for your emergency savings. You'll want this money to be available to you immediately without penalty or cost for withdrawals.

Begin to save a portion of your gross income (1-10%). One way to do this is to use automatic deductions from your paycheck. Save a small portion of all your income until your emergency fund reaches at least $1,000.

Remember, this is money you are not to spend, except in the case of an emergency or surprise expense. Wait until you have $1,000 saved for emergencies before paying off debts.

If you want to reach this goal faster, you should consider selling items around your home that you no longer use. Perhaps you can have a yard sale, or sell them on eBay or Craigslist. Try making a list of ways you can increase income, decrease expenses or raise cash by selling things. Don't forget other ways to save like couponing and carpooling.

Start giving regularly to the Lord

Your home church should be a great place to start your giving, and you may also have other ministries that you would like to support. You might not be able to give a full 10% of your gross income at this point, but you can always begin with 2%, 5%, etc.

Tips on Starting Tithing

- Consider giving first to the Lord before paying other bills.
- Commit to a percentage to tithe, and do it consistently.
- You might also want to give the same percent on bonuses, commissions, and other unexpected income.
- This will probably be a step of faith for you. It will be one that the Lord will honor.

"Will man rob God? Yet you are robbing me. But you say, 'How have we robbed you?' In your tithes and contributions."

(Malachi 3:8 ESV)

Grow as a Steward

Take a few minutes to be alone with God. Tell Him that in your heart you are transferring ownership of all your resources to Him. List the major items, if you find that helpful. Consider writing down your commitment in the journal pages for this section and dating it. Learn to say no to your desires to spend and yes to your desire to save.

Reward:

What did you decide to do to reward yourself for completing this goal? Be sure you have written this down on your Money Map and here:

_____

_____

_____

_____

_____

Devotional

Purposeful Obedience

"As obedient children, do not be conformed to the former lusts which were yours in your ignorance, but like the Holy One who called you, be holy yourselves also in all your behavior."

(1 Peter 1:14-15 NASB)

Sometimes it can be difficult to do the things we want to do. When we became Christians, God began to change us from the inside, as the Holy Spirit began moving in us, creating new hearts with new desires. As a new Christian, I surprised myself with the longing to be obedient to God in ways I'd never considered before. These longings changed the way I thought, and those new thoughts began to change the way I lived. Often, though, I found myself, like Paul, doing the things I didn't want to do and not doing the things I did want to do. My behavior frustrated and disappointed me, and I think many people are feeling the same frustration. One area is in stewardship. The Holy Spirit has placed a longing in our hearts to become good managers of what God has given us. We truly want to control our spending, give more to help others, get out of debt, and bring a balance into our financial lives. However, we find that the path to stewardship is difficult, and it's easy to stumble. I've learned that it's okay to stumble, because when we are aware of our shortcomings and turn to Him, He can work more powerfully through us. Being obedient means being willing to do what God's Word says—regardless of our preferences. Are there ways you have failed to be obedient to God that you want to confess? Pray about it now.

Larry Burkett
Scripture Reading: Nehemiah 1-5

Encouragement

God is faithful! He is our Provider! I was able to save up three months of living expenses for an emergency. I was laid off from work, but I had the extra money on hand. I continued to tithe and learned to pray more before I bought something. Learning to be content is important. God can be trusted in every situation. God blessed me with another job at the right time and at the right place four and a half months after I was laid off, and I still had extra money in the bank. Praise the Lord!

Kate

When my wife and I were first married, we often had small disagreements about how we should handle our finances. But, over time, those small disagreements became a big problem. Crown's tools and resources helped us to overcome our differences, and create a biblically based financial plan together. We were reminded that God is the creator and owner of all our resources. Actively preparing and planning a budget has helped our spiritual growth! We also realized that both husband and wife needed to be involved in the management of finances. I do the accounting, and she balances the checkbook.

Curt and Susan

Journal

_____

_____

_____

_____

_____

_____

_____

_____

_____

_____

Now hope that is seen is not hope. For who hopes for what he sees? But if we hope for what we do not see, we wait for it with patience.

Romans 8:24-25 ESV

_____

_____

_____

_____

_____

_____

_____

_____

_____

_____

_____

_____

The stingy are eager to get rich and are unaware that poverty awaits them.

Proverbs 28:22 NIV

_____

_____

_____

_____

_____

_____

_____

_____

_____

_____

_____

The plans of the diligent lead to profit as surely as haste leads to poverty.

Proverbs 21:5 NIV

SUGGESTED GUIDELINE PERCENTAGE FOR NET SPENDABLE INCOME

Housing	28 - 40%
Food	10 - 16%
Transportation	12 - 16%
Insurance	4 - 6%
Debt	0 - 6%
Entertainment/Recreation	2 - 8%
Clothing	4 - 8%
Savings	4 - 10%
Medical	4 - 8%
Miscellaneous	4 - 8%
Investments	0 - 8%
School/Child Care	0 - 8%
Maximum Total	100%

DESTINATION 2

PAY OFF CREDIT CARD DEBT

The borrower is slave to the lender.

PROVERBS 22:7 NIV

In This Destination...

1. Pay off credit cards

2. Increase savings to one month's living expenses

3. Increase giving to the Lord through your time, talents, and money

4. Look for creative ways to increase your income

DATE COMPLETED: _____

By now, you should have $1,000 in an Emergency Savings Account. Congratulations, you have completed Destination One and are on your way to reaching true financial freedom! Have you celebrated this achievement? Be sure and exercise the reward you built in for this victory and then set another reward for finishing Destination Two. Bear in mind this will be a bigger challenge than Destination One and thus should be a bigger reward!

Are you trapped by worldly goals?

These four symptoms are found in households suffering from economic crisis. Do you see any in your own life? Some people suffer these symptoms in order, while others may identify with just one or two. Following each symptom is a biblical attitude you will want to adopt to help you avoid ongoing financial crisis.

Symptom 1: I Am Struggling to Pay My Monthly Bills. Many families develop anxiety when they have built up more monthly costs than they can afford to pay. Between your mortgage or rent, car payments, insurance, and groceries, fixed costs can start to eat up a larger percentage of your budget than your income can handle.

Attitude: I Will Stop Borrowing

"The wicked borrows and does not pay back, but the righteous is gracious and gives."

Psalm 37:21 NASB

Scripture clearly indicates that borrowing is not normal to God's plan and was never intended to be used as a routine part of our financial planning. Borrowing denies you the opportunity to experience His overwhelming blessings in response to giving what is clearly within God's will. Make a commitment to stop borrowing money, and instead choose to live on what God provides.

Symptom 2: My Expenses Are Too Big for My Income, so a Bigger Income Must Be Needed. Sadly, the trend is that debt and spending tend to *increase*, not decrease, when income increases. Typically, within a year or less, the bills are larger than they were before, and the pressures are even greater. Now the extra income is necessary to survive.

Attitude: I Will Grow My Savings.

"There is precious treasure and oil in the dwelling of the wise, but a foolish man swallows it up."

Proverbs 21:20 NASB

Remember that the purpose of saving is to have extra resources to serve God and others so that He will be made known and honored. If your expenses are too big, you need to cut them down until they not only fit within your budget, but also leave enough room to save. By saving now, you will be prepared for future costs that might tempt you to use credit.

Symptom 3: I Can't Stand This Pressure! I'll Buy Something New. Usually by the time you reach this symptom, your cars, appliances, and house are needing repairs. Plus, if you are married, marital pressures are reaching a boiling point. The logical thing to do seems to be to buy a new car or take a vacation to "get away from it all." Unfortunately, it always gets worse later. Getting into new debt, or breaking your budget to splurge on desires, will only add to your economic crisis.

Attitude: I Will Not Make Hasty Decisions.

"The plans of the diligent lead surely to advantage, but everyone who is hasty comes surely to poverty."

Proverbs 21:5 NASB

Patience and consistency, rather than quick decisions and instant success, are the ways to financial security. Prayerfully submit spending decisions to God, and then freely enjoy whatever God allows you to purchase.

Symptom 4: Going Through Divorce or Bankruptcy. Once the financial pressures build, the marital pressures build as well. It's difficult to have much communication when all you ever talk about are problems. For a few families, bankruptcy seems to be the solution, so they liquidate the debts and begin again. Within a short period of time many of these couples face the same symptoms that prompted the bankruptcy.

Attitude: I Will Stick to My Budget.

"Poverty and shame will come to him who neglects discipline, but he who regards reproof will be honored."

Proverbs 13:18 NASB

We should all learn to live on a reasonable budget. Overspending should be so discouraged in Christian homes that we wouldn't even consider it a possibility. We have to be consistent in our daily disciplines and remain dedicated to achieving our goals. But more than that, we need to know and follow God's way if we are ever to know true financial freedom. How we handle money is an outside indicator of our inward spiritual condition.

PRACTICAL TOOLS

Your goal in this destination is to pay off all your credit card debt. Why just credit card debt? Because it is typically the most expensive debt that you have. By paying off expensive debt, you can make rapid progress towards having more income available to pay off other debts.

Pay off credit cards

The first step is to stop borrowing (using your credit cards) and develop a debt payoff plan.

Use the Debt Snowball Calculator to create a plan that uses the rollover method to decrease the amount of total interest you will have to pay along with the life of your loan. This tool will help you choose which cards to pay off first. You can also accelerate your debt reduction if you put extra income (ex: bonuses, raises, unexpected income, etc.) toward your debt payoff plan. Visit crown.org/debtsnowball

---

Remember: The money you were setting aside to increase your emergency funds to $1,000 can now be designated for Destination 2.

You will probably want to split this money between paying off credit cards, increasing saving, and giving. However, you might want to focus on the credit cards and giving first.

Through all this, maintain your emergency savings to be at least $1,000.

Think about seeking counsel and assistance. Through Crown, you can work with a MoneyLife Mentor who will personally walk you through this and any other destination of the Money Map. Visit http://mentoring.crown.org

Increase savings to one month living expenses

Revisit the Savings Calculator to determine a new amount to save each month. Visit www.crown.org/savings

Remember to plan for major repairs (ex: auto, appliances, housing, etc.) as you save.

Note: your "living expenses" are only a portion of your spending plan. If you lost your job and had no income, what expenses would you delete or reduce from your spending plan? Think about eating out, subscriptions, or even items like income tax that you would not have to pay. The non-negotiable, "bare bones" items that are left are what make up your actual living expenses.

Increase giving to the Lord through your time, talents, and money

Consider volunteering a portion of your time each week at your church or a ministry you are passionate about. Take time to pray about increasing your percentage giving at this point.

Look for creative ways to increase your income

You may want to consider a part-time job or a side job like cutting your neighbor's lawn, pet sitting, repairing friends' cars on the weekend, etc. If you do take on more work, be careful to keep balance in your life. Don't sacrifice your family time. And if both spouses are considering working, make sure it makes sense financially and emotionally to have two incomes.

Grow as a Steward

God is eager to bless generous, open-hearted people. The miracle is that He is even eager to forgive greedy, tightfisted, self-indulgent people and help them change. Through the wonder of grace, it is possible for us to become not only debt-free but to be able to lend generously. Right now, ask God to enable you to become a person who lends liberally but does not borrow.

Reward:

What did you decide to do to reward yourself for completing this goal? Be sure you have written this down on your Money Map and here:

_____

_____

_____

_____

_____

Devotional

Time to Choose

Some choices are hard, tempting us to delay them indefinitely if we could. We rest a foot on both sides of a line we largely ignore, arguing that it's fuzzy.

Jesus told us to put God first in our lives, to love Him with all our heart, soul, mind, and strength (Mark 12:30). But He knew our tendency to rationalize, to manipulate God's law until it conforms to our desires. Peering into our heart and seeking out true priorities, He used scalpel precision to pinpoint His greatest competitor for our devotion.

Who – me in love with money?

Money, unsurrendered, is often a ticket to power and pride, values for which Satan rebelled. Jesus makes the choice very clear: It is impossible for us to serve money—even in a small way—and still serve God.

The Crusaders of the 12th century hired mercenaries to fight for them. Because it was a religious war, the mercenaries were first baptized. As they went under the water, they would hold their swords up out of the water as a statement that they—not Jesus—would be in control of their weapons.

Unfortunately, many people today hold their wallet or purse out of the water. In their desire for control, they think they can straddle the line, but Jesus knows exactly who—or what—comes first.

Scripture Reading: Matthew 6:19-24

Encouragement

When I first heard about Crown Financial Ministries, I was hoping that God would make a way for me to eliminate my debts—around $20,000 by that time. It took a little while for me to understand that it was my responsibility to take control over the financial mess that I was in, but I was really determined to make the necessary changes.

I bought several Christian books about finances, I studied them, I believed in God's promises, I asked friends to pray with me, I made radical changes in my lifestyle, I budgeted, I got control over emotional spending, I cut all my credit cards off, I made agreements with the creditors, I honored the agreements, I got a second job, I moved over to a friend's house, I cried a lot, and three and a half years later I became debt free! I am still living under the grace of this freedom.

-Rachel

For the past couple of years, I had been finding pleasure and comfort in shopping and purchasing items I couldn't afford to buy. It felt good to buy something new in the moment, but later I would feel guilty. This cycle continued for many months until my *husband and I finally resolved to get out of debt as quickly as we could. Our major debt was the credit card, around $8,000; a daunting sum. We spent several months putting most of our extra money on the credit card, and saving some of it for emergencies. It's hard to make a lot of progress with those interest rates, and it was discouraging to see how long it would take us to be free from the burden of debt. Last month my husband did our taxes, and praise God! We received a tax return large enough to eradicate our debt! What a blessing! We didn't think we could pay it off before the year was over, and now we're free!*

-Tim and Julia

Journal

_____

_____

_____

_____

_____

_____

_____

_____

_____

_____

No servant can serve two masters, for either he will hate the one and love the other, or he will be devoted to the one and despise the other. You cannot serve God and money.

Luke 16:13 ESV

_____

_____

_____

_____

_____

_____

_____

_____

_____

_____

Do your planning and prepare your fields before building your house.

Proverbs 24:27 NLT

_____

_____

_____

_____

_____

_____

_____

_____

_____

_____

The rich rules over the poor and the borrower is slave to the lender.

Proverbs 22:7 ESV

PAY OFF ANY OTHER CONSUMER DEBT

Keep out of debt and owe no man anything.

ROMANS 13:8 NASB

Paying off your credit card debt (or having stayed out of it completely) is an amazing accomplishment! Congratulations on conquering one of the most difficult stages of the Money Map. Your choices are opening your life to the Lord's blessings. Plan your reward for this next stage, and begin to map out how you will leave almost all of your debt behind.

In This Destination...

1. Pay off all consumer debts

2. Increase savings to 3 months' living expenses

3. Increase giving to the Lord's work

DATE COMPLETED:_____

Compared to the rest of the world, almost every single American lives an affluent life. An affluent way of life is a mixed blessing. On the positive side, our prosperity has made life much easier and has freed a great deal of money to spread God's Word. But on the negative side, prosperity requires a great deal of time and attention. In fact, the urgency of our materialistic lifestyles becomes a tyranny that demands most of our energy.

The American dream only a couple of decades ago was a good job, a comfortable home, and a nice car. Today, it has become guaranteed employment, retirement plans, a home, two cars, a summer cottage, and college educations for all the kids. The possession of "things" has become the scorecard to determine "success."

A survey of the scriptural warnings about riches and their dangers might suggest that we should avoid all luxuries. That simply is not true. God does not prohibit us from enjoying the benefits of this world (after all, they are His)! Rather, He tells us not to get entangled in them to the point that we are no longer able to fulfill our primary purpose—to serve Him. The real purpose of our resources is to free us to do more for Christ, not less.

These are five dangers of prosperity to guard against, followed by Scripture that will help you establish a balance in the area of material "things."

1. Adjusting to a life of indulgence as normal. It is amazing that in less than fifty years we have grown to accept guaranteed salaries, insurance for every contingency, retirement benefits, and two-car families as normal. When the economy couldn't supply those things quickly enough, we simply mortgaged our future generations to pay for them. That selfishness is short-lived, because eventually we borrow more than can ever be repaid. But the real reason this debt-funded economy always fails is because it violates basic biblical principles.

"A faithful man will abound with blessings, but he who makes haste to be rich will not go unpunished."

Proverbs 28:20 NASB

2. Focusing on worldly success. For people who have committed themselves to an eternity with God, it's amazing how worldly our value system has become. Obviously, many Christians are financially and spiritually mature, but when we judge people on the basis of financial success, we confuse riches with spirituality. Oftentimes we wrongly label people who are not financially successful as less spiritual. God never shows us that those who are poor cannot also be spiritually rich—just look at the Apostles.

"To this present hour we are both hungry and thirsty, and are poorly clothed, and are roughly treated, and are homeless."

1 Corinthians 4:11 NASB

3. Dulling God's direction. Nothing prohibits Christians from obeying God more than the tug of material comforts. Once we have adjusted to a lifestyle that includes many comforts, it is very difficult to surrender them to serve God. God can and does use Christians everywhere. But in order to be used by God in any capacity, a Christian must be willing to serve God no matter what the costs.

4. Adopting an attitude of superiority. You would think that knowing everything belongs to God would make even the wealthiest among us humble. But it's sad what a little bit of material success will do to our ego and pride. Those who have been given responsibility in this life must be very careful to exercise it with great caution, lest they give up their eternal rewards for some temporary ones.

5. Indifference toward the needs of others. A real danger of material affluence is that we begin to think everybody has it. But that's simply not true. The vast majority of people in this world go to bed hungry and wake up hungry. Let me assure you that most of them aren't lazy or evil—they are poor. They are the ones that Christ describes in Matthew 25:45. Giving to feed the poor and homeless is a command, not a request.

There must always be a balance in the area of material "things." So how can we reach that balance between using material things and being controlled by them? Let's look at Scripture.

Remember Solomon, a man who had everything this world had to offer. In 1 Kings 3:5, we read, "At Gibeon the Lord appeared to Solomon during the night in a dream, and God said, 'Ask for whatever you want me to give you.'"

Imagine this happening to you or me! How would you answer?

Solomon answered in 1 Kings 3:9-14, "'So give your servant a discerning heart to govern your people and to distinguish between right and wrong. For who is able to govern this great people of yours?'

"The Lord was pleased that Solomon had asked for this. So God said to him, 'Since you have asked for this and not for long life or wealth for yourself, nor have asked for the death of your enemies but for discernment in administering justice, I will do what you have asked. I will give you a wise and discerning heart, so that there will never have been anyone like you, nor will there ever be.

"Moreover, I will give you what you have not asked for—both wealth and honor—so that in your lifetime you will have no equal among kings. And if you walk in obedience to me and keep my decrees and commands as David your father did, I will give you a long life'" (NIV).

Solomon later wrote in Proverbs 3:13-14, "Blessed are those who find wisdom, those who gain understanding, for she is more profitable than silver and yields better returns than gold" (NIV).

One way to avoid the dangers of prosperity is to heed Solomon's advice in this passage. God's Word recommends we change our desires from wanting to become rich to seeking the true riches of His Kingdom, just as Solomon did.

PRACTICAL TOOLS

Pay off all consumer debt (auto, furniture, student loans, etc.)

Now that your credit cards are paid off, you can begin to eliminate other types of debt!

Look to Navient or Nelnet to renegotiate your student loans or to defer payments. You can also look for student loan information on the Crown website.

www.crown.org/education-plan

Visit the Debt Snowball Calculator, and make a debt payoff plan for your consumer debt. Remember that you can accelerate your debt reduction if you put extra income (ex: bonuses, raises, unexpected income, etc.) toward your plan. For extra help planning to pay off your car, use one of Crown's automobile calculators. Visit www.crown.org/auto

Increase savings to 3 months' living expenses

Imagine the relief you will feel once you reach this goal, and start thinking of the ways you will be able to honor God as your family's finances become more stable! Before you begin working towards this goal, visit the savings calculator to determine a new amount to save each month. Remember to plan for major repairs (ex. auto, appliances, housing, etc.).

Tips to stay out of automobile debt:

- Pay off your car loan and keep your car at least three more years.
- After your last car loan payment, keep making the payment, but pay it to yourself.
- When you are ready to replace your car, saved cash plus your car's trade-in value (or even better, what you can sell it for) should be sufficient to buy a car without credit.

Increase giving to the Lord's work

- Consider volunteering a portion of your time each week at your church or a ministry you are passionate about.
- Pray about increasing your percentage giving at this point. Aim for your giving to be at or above 10% of your gross income.
- Make sure you are giving to a reputable organization. Visit Charity Navigator's website to learn more about almost any non-profit.
- If you have benefitted from the work of a non-profit, highly consider giving back through volunteering or donating.

Grow as a Steward

Copy Proverbs 3:27 onto a card: "Do not withhold good from those to whom it is due, when it is in your power to do it" (NASB). Pray over this verse and all of your creditors. Think about what it will require of you to do good to each of these persons or groups. Ask God what you should do. Pray for each of your creditors, envisioning each one as a real person.

Reward:

What did you decide to do to reward yourself for completing this goal? Be sure you have written this down on your Money Map and here:

_____

_____

_____

_____

_____

Devotional

Deceitfulness of Riches

"There is one who pretends to be rich, but has nothing; Another pretends to be poor, but has great wealth."

Proverbs 13:7 NASB

Old man Cates was a very rich man—one of the richest in the islands. He had a sizable plantation and prospered financially from its produce; but he had few friends. He was very tight with his money, and the wages he paid his hired labor were low. Over the years he spent little and amassed quite a savings. And through those years he didn't have time for God; he was too busy building "bigger barns." After many years, old man Cates became extremely ill. Because he suffered from pain that hindered his sleep, he often rocked during the evenings. His condition grew worse until it was evident that he wouldn't live. One evening, hearing his screams, his wife ran to him and heard him cry out, "Oh, my God! Jesus of Nazareth has passed me by!" With that on his lips, he died. Time ran out for the man who had no time for God. The expression of terrible fright remained on his face and the sounds of his agonizing cries about the intense heat of the fire into which he was passing haunted his wife. Just like the rich man of Luke 16, old man Cates would have traded his wealth for Lazarus' poverty, if he had only realized the deceitfulness of his riches. We need to remind ourselves that we cannot trust in riches. Only our trust in Christ will secure our future—now and in the hereafter.

Larry Burkett

Scripture Reading: Revelation 10-14

Encouragement

When my husband and I were married, we realized individually we had made a mess of our finances and together we faced a mountain of combined debt. We had over $21,000 in credit card debt, two car loans, a student loan, and now a home mortgage. A couple in our church introduced us to Crown and helped us get started on a budget.

We figured with what we were able to put towards debt that we could pay off our credit card debt in five years. God's math ended up working better than ours. In just two years we had paid off all of our credit card debt, the student loan, and one of the car loans. Today we are able to live on one income, and I am able to stay at home with our daughter.

\- Marcus and Elizabeth

God called me to my doctoral work, and I knew that I had to be obedient, but I never once thought to pray about loans or other sources of support. After I defended my dissertation, I took a look at my finances and was horrified! I had no savings and was living off the last of my loan. I didn't know how I was going make ends meet.

I began to use Crown, and I put all of my mistakes, financial and otherwise, as well as my hopes and dreams before the Lord. I asked Him to fix what was broken inside me so that I would not only see that all that I had was from Him, but to never again take advantage of His grace by gaining debt. Not only was I able to make ends meet during the summer after I graduated, I was able to tithe, begin early payments on my student loans, and pay all the extra moving expenses that the University did not provide! I have paid off two of my credit cards, paid over my student loan amount each month, and have started a savings account.

- Susannah

Journal

_____

_____

_____

_____

_____

_____

_____

_____

_____

Owe no one anything, except to love each other, for the one who loves another has fulfilled the law.

Romans 13:8 NASB

_____

_____

_____

_____

_____

_____

_____

_____

_____

The Lord will open to you his good treasury, the heavens, to give the rain to your land in its season and to bless all the work of your hands. And you shall lend to many nations, but you shall not borrow.

Deuteronomy 28:12 ESV

_____

_____

_____

_____

_____

_____

_____

_____

_____

_____

_____

The wicked borrows but does not pay back, but the righteous is generous and gives.

Psalm 37:21 ESV

DESTINATION 4

ADJUST YOUR PLAN

"For I know the plans I have for you," declares the Lord, "plans to prosper you and not to harm you, plans to give you hope and a future."

JEREMIAH 29:11 NIV

You are a third of a way to true financial freedom! With your debts paid off, you are well on your way to being able to be an excellent steward of all of your resources. During this stage, you will reexamine your goals and long-term plans. As you work through Destination Four, spend time in the Lord's Word and in prayer as you seek His guidance for your life. Once again, congratulations!

1. Adjust your spending plan accordingly

2. Start saving for major purchases

3. Start saving for retirement

4. Increase savings to 6 months' living expenses

5. Retake your MLI assessment and revisit your goals

DATE COMPLETED: _____

How to define success

Today, we often look first at someone's bank account to determine if they are successful. Most of those we call successful today are frustrated and miserable people with terrible family lives. Many "successful" people participate in extreme and dangerous behavior because they are searching or feel as though they have nothing. Sometimes the worst thing that can happen to those without Christ is for them to accomplish their goals, because they turn out to be so worthless.

Obviously, Christians don't fall into the same traps set by Satan, do they? Unfortunately, Christians do fall into these traps. Why? Because the lies are so convincing that we believe they have to be true.

The norm taught in God's Word is either enough or an abundance for those who believe and follow (Psalm 37:25; Proverbs 3:18; Proverbs 10:3; Proverbs 13:22; Matthew 13:12; Mark 11:24; Luke 6:38). There is a great danger in seeing God only from worldly eyes. Then all riches and all blessings are measured in terms of what God can do for us, rather than what we can do for God.

To be a spiritual success, a Christian must be willing to give up their rights and accept God's plan. Out of necessity, God will place believers at every tier in society to minister to those around them. "So then it does not depend on the man who wills or the man who runs, but on God who has mercy" (Romans 9:16 NASB).

Does god want me to be poor?

Since the world puts so much emphasis on material success, many Christians have naturally concluded that the opposite of that must be God's way, and Christians should be poor. Or if they aren't poor, at least they ought to look that way. Satan is tricky. Those that he can't trap into his plan, he tries to drive through and out the other side. He warps one of God's blessings so that God's people will be careful to avoid it. Poverty is a reality in Scripture, but it certainly is not a promise. God said there would always be poor in the land, but He never said they would be His people. When God chose someone to live on limited resources, it was either to teach that person a lesson or to use him as an example. Many Christians believe that giving up something makes them spiritual. Although they may not believe they "earned" their salvation, they now believe that by self-sacrifice they must earn God's acceptance.

Riches syndrome

Other Christians have concluded that since poverty isn't normal, then riches must be. They, therefore, have assumed that God must make them wealthy to protect His image. They will attempt to glorify God by getting rich in a completely secular way. Others try to manipulate God to work for them. They give, but usually to get. They continually demand more and the best, while constantly trying to convince others that this is normal. Rarely, if ever, do they stop to consider God's plan for fear that it won't coincide with their concept of prosperity.

PRACTICAL TOOLS

Adjust your spending plan accordingly

Congratulations! You've made major progress to get to Destination Four where you evaluate how you are doing. Compare your current spending plan with the guideline percentages on page 25. Are you on track? Do you need to adjust your categories or percentages? Are there ways you can increase giving, debt reduction, and savings?

Start saving for major purchases

Home

The most expensive purchase you will most likely ever make will be your house. As you begin to save for this occasion consider:

- Is it better to buy or rent? Check your spending plan to see what you can afford.
- Is your job secure enough to take on a mortgage or higher rent payment?
- How long do you plan to live in the area?
- What is the economy like? You do not want to be stuck with a home you cannot sell because of a poor economy.
- What is the cost of living? Even moving from one county to another could cause changes.

Saving for Major Home or Appliance Replacements and Repairs

Evaluate the timing of when appliances or repairs may be anticipated, and save accordingly. Put 4% of your mortgage payment into a savings account for home repairs.

Cars and Transportation

Another major expense to plan for is buying a car. Examine your motives and make sure you are buying a car because it suits your needs, not your desires. After assessing your needs, if you discover you really do need to purchase a car, consider buying one that is used.

Only purchase a car after getting the most out of your existing car. And when you do go shopping, look for the best value, which is not necessarily the lowest price.

When you're ready to buy, pay in cash. However, if you must borrow, arrange for a simple interest loan from a bank or another financial institution, not the dealership. Make sure your loan has no payoff restrictions. Finally, sell your old car yourself instead of trading it in.

Starting Your Own Business

Is God leading you to devote your time, talent, and treasure towards working for yourself rather than others? If you want to start saving up to start your own business, seek wise counsel and be sure not to mix your personal finances with your business finances. You can learn more about starting a business venture at www.crownbiz.com.

Start saving for retirement

There are many different retirement plans, and there is not one "best" plan that is guaranteed to work for everyone.

The best retirement investment that will fit into any retirement plan is to have a debt-free home. If you have a mortgage, pay it off as soon as possible. Then, use the money that was paying mortgage payments to start a retirement account or to reinforce an existing one.

As you start to save, ask yourself:
1. Why should I retire?
2. What will I do?
3. What if my retirement plan fails?
4. What if I can't retire?

Be a wise steward of your money. Trust in God and do not hoard your wealth. If you begin at a young age, be careful you do not sacrifice basic needs for the sake of retirement speculations. You don't need to try to protect against every eventuality. Take time to pray and plan for the future. Spouses should pray together about their retirement future and then trust God, who is "able to make all grace abound to you, so that always having all sufficiency in everything, you may have an abundance for every good deed" (2 Corinthians 9:8 NASB). Together, you can establish financial goals and work towards them.

Start saving early, especially if your employer offers a matching contribution to your 401k or 403b. When it comes to investments, remember that they are for the long-term. Diversify them, but always make sure that they align with your values. As you make these choices, seek godly counsel, such as Kingdom Advisors or Sound Mind Investing.

In this economic environment, it is important to consider postponing the age of retirement to the latest possible date that your health will allow. Plan to work in some capacity, keeping in mind it may not be your current job. After retiring, mentor younger people in the field of your expertise to pass on your knowledge and wise counsel.

Increase savings to 6 months' living expenses

Continue to grow your savings. Revisit the Savings Goal calculator. Remember that this money is to be kept in an account that you can easily withdraw from without a fee. Visit www.crown.org/savings

Retake your MoneyLife® Indicator assessment and revisit your goals

Compare your first MLI report (at the start of the Money Map) to the results of this report. Do you see improvement? Are there any surprises?

Determine your revised financial goals—especially for your 3 lowest scores—and record each goal in all 9 key areas of beliefs and behaviors.

Grow as a Steward

Choose a week to pay attention to how you handle situations that involve money. Watch for attitudes that seem characteristic of you. Maybe it's when you go bargain hunting at the grocery store. Maybe you'll get your bank statement and put it away without looking at it. Perhaps you'll argue with someone over money, or perhaps you'll buy a gift you feel is extravagant. Afterward, write down what you did, how you felt, and what you wanted to accomplish. Did you feel excited, angry, frustrated, affectionate, determined, or scared? Maybe you were aware of feeling nothing at all. What was your goal? Were you trying to make ends meet, please someone else, serve God, or do something nice for yourself?

If it's hard to identify your motives, that's okay. This doesn't come naturally for all of us. But do make note of the situation.

Devotional

Priceless Bread

"I have learned to be content whatever the circumstances."

Philippians 4:11 NIV

The best things in life, including contentment, cannot be bought.

Contentment requires freedom from both fear and greed. Recognizing God as the provider of our needs frees us from fear. Recognizing Him as the owner of everything frees us from greed.

As our provider, God is totally predictable in His faithfulness to provide and totally unpredictable in His creative methods.

When World War II drew to a close, many malnourished, fearful orphans were placed in camps where, despite excellent care, they still slept poorly. An understanding doctor began giving each child a piece of bread at bedtime—not to eat, just to hold. Any hungry children could get more to eat, but when they were finished, they would still have this piece of bread just to hold.

The children began to sleep peacefully, knowing they would have food to eat the next day.

God has given us His guarantee—our "piece of bread."

"And my God will meet all your needs according to His glorious riches."

Philippians 4:19 NIV

As we cling to His promise of provision, recognizing His ownership and control, we can relax and be content "whatever the circumstances."

Scripture Reading: Philippians 4:11-13, 19

Encouragement

Over the past 5 years we have seen God eradicate $84,000 of debt. Now we have no debt, our giving has increased, our savings have increased, and more importantly we have learned how to be good stewards of all that God has blessed us with. Our next financial goal is to build our house without debt. While this seems impossible to most people in our culture, we know that we serve a God who provides all that we need. Should we someday have a house, this house will be a testimony of what God can do when we are obedient to Him.

For those of you still on this journey, trust in God, honor God in all your deeds, and keep up the steady-plodding.

-Matthew and Irene

I used to work as a petroleum engineer on rigs around the world. After using Crown, I realized God's part in my finances. I assessed my savings and decided to leave the oil industry. After taking the Crown class, I recognized for the first time that what I had put away was enough, and I didn't have to keep working. I had always handled my money conservatively and responsibly, but the scriptural focus of Crown gave me a new perspective. I used to think the point of life was always to work hard to save money for the future. I defined a successful career as having a good salary and managing it correctly. I just didn't relate that to God. Now I work in ministry, and I walk in every day and say, "OK, God, this is your ministry, and I'm here for you."

- Lisa

Journal

_____

_____

_____

_____

_____

_____

_____

_____

_____

_____

The Lord does not let the righteous go hungry, but he thwarts the craving of the wicked.

Proverbs 10:3 NIV

_____

_____

_____

_____

_____

_____

_____

_____

_____

_____

A faithful man will be richly blessed, but one eager to get rich will not go unpunished.

Proverbs 28:20 NIV

_____

_____

_____

_____

_____

_____

_____

_____

_____

_____

Wealth gained hastily will dwindle, but whoever gathers little by little will increase it.

Proverbs 13:11 ESV

SAVE FOR THE FUTURE

Steady plodding brings prosperity.

PROVERBS 21:5 TLB

In This Destination

1. Continue saving for major purchases and retirement

2. Continue saving up to 12 months' of living expenses

3. Create education/college funds for each child

4. Increase giving to the Lord's work

DATE COMPLETED:_____

Hopefully completing Destination Four was refreshing and eye opening as you move into the last stages of the Money Map. In this step, you will prepare for Destinations Six and Seven. As you do, remember that your journey does not stop when you finish the Money Map. Your journey to becoming a good steward and achieving true financial freedom continues even after your departure from this Earth! You have the ability to make an impact for the Lord which will last for generations.

How much is enough?

How can you tell when your finances are in balance? When are you accumulating too much? When have you stepped over the range of provision and begun to protect rather than provide?

How much should you leave your children? How much should you invest for retirement?

When making these decisions, keep these factors in mind:
- God's plan for your life
- Present spending level
- Future income potential
- Dependability of present income
- Potential vocational changes.

A Christian businessman once asked a very pertinent question: "I have a surplus of money each year. What am I to do with it: give it away, invest it, put it into a retirement plan, or what?" On the surface, the Scriptures would seem to be confusing on this issue. One proverb says a wise man has a surplus in his home, while a fool has bare cupboards. However, another says that a poor man has God's blessings, and a rich man is a fool. Even the parables of Christ would appear somewhat confusing. In one parable He rebuked a rich fool who built larger barns to store his surplus, and in another He rebuked the man who failed to invest a large surplus wisely.

There is one absolute that helps to answer confusing questions: God's Word is always right and is never in conflict! God is always dealing with heart attitudes. We might call them motives. In each situation the motives must be analyzed. For one person, a surplus of money represents a trust from God that can be used for current and future needs. For another, it represents a trap of Satan to lead him out of God's path. The certainty is that Scripture warns that there is a greater danger in having a surplus than in having a need.

Retirement provision is something that confuses many Christians. Who can best provide for your retirement years: God or man? Begin to assess right now how much you will really need later. Reassess your need for retirement and take a portion of what you don't consider necessary and give it to the Lord's ministry today. God will provide for the Christian with the right attitude.

Inheritance

Another area of Christian finances that is widely misunderstood is inheritance. It's important to remember that the most important inheritance we can offer our children is a godly influence that leads to salvation.

A brief survey of the Bible reveals that God provided for each generation through inheritance. In biblical times, the sons inherited their father's properties and thus provided for the rest of their family.

> *"A good man leaves an inheritance to his children's children, and the wealth of the sinner is stored up for the righteous."*
>
> Proverbs 13:22 NASB

Prepare those to whom you will leave your inheritance. To explain the great importance of this concept, let me share this story.

One man I was counseling had accumulated a sizable estate. When I asked him what he planned to do with it all, he said, "I'll leave it to my children, I guess." I asked him why he didn't just give it to them right then, and he replied, "Why, they don't know how to handle money; they'd just lose it all." When asked if he thought they wouldn't lose it after he died, his response was, "Well, I'll be gone then, so who cares?" I discussed with him that God wants us to be a good steward even after our death.

Take time to prepare those to whom you will leave your inheritance. Some Christians are superstitious without realizing it and avoid discussing death for fear that it will happen. This I can say with certainty—unless the Lord comes first, it will happen for each of us. Talking about death neither hastens nor delays it; it only makes it easier for those left behind.

PRACTICAL TOOLS

Continue saving for major purchases and retirement

Allocate your savings according to your goals and reevaluate your planned major purchases by asking these questions:

1. Is it necessary?
2. Does it reflect my Christian ethic?
3. Does my spouse agree with this purchase?
4. Does it add to or detract from my family?
5. What will the upkeep costs be, and can I afford them?

As you continue saving for retirement, make sure to prepare your family. If you are married, each spouse should be fully trained in all financial matters. Don't put off creating a will or a trust. For more resources visit www.crown.org/plan-your-legacy

Continue saving up to 12 months of living expenses

Re-evaluate and make a plan for what you will use your savings on. Be careful to not dip into your savings for investments or impulse buys. Research if your current savings account is still the best for you. Compound interest is your friend. You can greatly increase your savings by taking advantage of this tool.

There are also ways to save other than just in your bank account. Consider building up your pantry with non-perishable food and having a water supply in case of emergencies.

Create education/college funds for each child

Prayerfully consider the best educational path for your children. Do not be swayed by the current trend that every child has to go to an expensive, private school. There are many paths to an excellent education and career.

Encourage your child to put thought into their future plans. The Career Direct Assessment is an online service that helps students uncover God's unique design for them and learn what type of education and career would allow them to fill their perfect role in His Kingdom. By going into college with a solid idea of what degree they would work towards, your child can avoid additional tuition by graduating on time or early. This tool was created to help students be excellent stewards by guiding them to use God's resources for a degree that will help them to impact others instead of misusing money on a degree that will leave them spiritually unsatisfied.

As your family considers what type of education is best, you can simultaneously be saving for the occasion. There are many ways to lower tuition costs. For example, your child could earn college credits before even graduating from high school. See if your child would be interested in taking AP classes or CLEP courses. Your student could knock off a semester or even a year of college expenses by earning credits this way.

It's also a myth that having a part-time or summer job detracts from a student's grades. Many students can work part-time or over the summer and use their earnings toward their spending expenses or tuition in college. This will also instill responsibility in them and help them to learn to take ownership over their finances.

Increase giving to the Lord's work

Reconsider what needs God has put on your heart through prayer and time in His Word. Continue giving until those needs are met. Remember that you cannot and do not need to meet every need in the world, only those which God has shared with you. If you can, increase your tithe. You may also want to look into asset giving.

Grow as a Steward

Consider the following passage:

"Once again I saw that nothing on earth makes sense. For example, some people don't have friends or family. But they are never satisfied with what they own, and they never stop working to get more. They should ask themselves, 'Why am I always working to have more? Who will get what I leave behind?' What a senseless and miserable life!" (Ecclesiastes 4:7-8 CEV)

This assessment also could apply to hoarding riches for a family. We are guardians of our families, but if we attempt to protect them from the testing and character building that will bring them to maturity in Christ, we do them great disservice.

Write out the top three items you think of for each of these categories:

1. Major purchases you would like to make over the next several decades
2. Things you want to leave your family
3. Goals for your retirement plan

Pray over this list (feel free to include more than three in each category), and ask God, "Will these things bring You glory?" Ask the Lord to bring you clarity, and determine whether or not you are planning to hoard treasures here on earth, or if you will be using your money and resources to build treasures in Heaven.

Reward: What did you decide to do to reward yourself for completing this goal? Be sure you have written this down on your Money Map and here:

_____

_____

_____

_____

_____

_____

Devotional

The Trust Factor

"Trust in the Lord with all your heart and lean not on your own understanding; in all your ways acknowledge Him, and He will make your paths straight."

Proverbs 3:5-6 NIV

Whom do you trust?

Scripture provides an accurate picture of who God is as well as what He wants for you and from you. This requires you to make a decision. Do you trust Him? Really?

It may sound simple, but it's not easy. It is probably the single most important question you will ever ask yourself. You had to answer it at one level when you chose to become a follower of Christ. Now you discover that you will continue to answer it at ever-increasing levels the rest of your life.

In many of our daily decisions God is asking, "Do you trust Me? Where are your limits?"

Most of us subconsciously draw lines that say, "I trust you this far but not way out in the dark where I can't see."

Think about it: How many choices do you have?

You can trust:

- The deceptions of the enemy
- The crowd
- Your own judgment
- The wisdom of the Creator

Be like Joshua who declared his trust as he immortalized the words, "But as for me and my household, we will serve the Lord" (NIV).

Scripture Reading: 2 Corinthians 1:8-10

Encouragement

My parents always taught me how to work hard and earn money, for that I am grateful! The one key missing though was how to save *it. That was introduced to me by Crown Financial Ministries. I feel bad I was not taught earlier, but better late than never! To share just a few accomplishments we have achieved by handling our money God's way:*

1. We put our four children through college. On graduation day, we surprised them—we gave them the gift of paying off their college loans. Each child had no idea we were going to do this! The tears and joy were worth every penny we worked to save for that moment.

2. We took time to save up for major purchases. Because of that, we were able to pay for all three of our daughters' weddings!

Years ago, before Crown, I would have thought all of the above things would be impossible. But we truly learned to trust God and set a goal. God was and will always be faithful. Some people might think we must have been rich to do all that, but we're not. We just learned how to save and budget. Praise God for His financial principles and His gifts to us!

-Madeline and Paul

We began our marriage 12 years ago with over sixty thousand dollars in student loan debt and assumed more debt from there. My husband and I committed to follow the Crown Money Map and pursue living debt free. We faced a crossroads in life though when we realized how much time we were spending working and were not able to spend with our two young children. It was at that point that we told God we would go wherever He led our family—we just wanted to know we were in His will. Two weeks later my husband was told about a position that had opened up for a camp director at a Christian camp nearby. It was through our Father bringing us to camp that we were able to pay off all of our debts. We are now on Destination 5 on the Money Map. God is faithful!

-Justin and Penelope

Journal

_____

_____

_____

_____

_____

_____

_____

_____

_____

_____

Live in harmony with one another. Do not be haughty, but associate with the lowly. Never be wise in your own sight.

Psalm 10:14 ESV

_____

_____

_____

_____

_____

_____

_____

_____

_____

_____

_____

But you, God, see the trouble of the afflicted; you consider their grief and take it in hand. The victims commit themselves to you; you are the helper of the fatherless.

Proverbs 28:20 NIV

_____

_____

_____

_____

_____

_____

_____

_____

_____

_____

_____

I rejoice in following your statutes as one rejoices in great riches.

Psalm 119:14 NIV

INVEST WISELY

Invest in seven ventures, yes, in eight; you do not know what disaster may come upon the land.

ECCLESIASTES 11:2 NIV

Making it to Destination Six is a major accomplishment! You should feel more free in your finances to follow the Lord wherever He leads you and also feel secure in your prayerfully laid-out plans and goals for your future. As you move forward, start thinking about sharing the joy that you have found through your journey to true financial freedom with others.

In This Destination

1. Buy affordable home

2. Begin prepaying home mortgage

3. Diversify investments

4. Increase giving to the Lord's work

DATE COMPLETED:_____

Why should Christians invest?

Once a faithful Christian friend asked: "Why should we help rich people get richer?" The obvious answer is that teaching Christians to invest wisely is as necessary as teaching them to budget. God has commissioned us to help Christians be better stewards, and that includes using surplus resources properly. In a very practical way, it is obvious that those with a surplus are able to give more to God's work than others are.

There are several legitimate reasons for a Christian to invest:

First, to further God's work. Some Christians have received a gift of giving (Romans 12:8). To them, the multiplication of material worth is an extension of their basic ministry within the Body of Christ. Even to those who do not have a gift of giving, investments are a way to preserve and multiply a surplus that has been provided for a later time.

Second, family responsibility. We are admonished to provide for those within our own households (1 Timothy 5:8). That provision was never limited to a person's life span. It extended to providing for your family even after your death. Not everyone can meet every need their family has, but if those who are able can meet their own family's needs, the church can concentrate on the needs of the poor.

Third, future needs. If parents believe that God wants their children to go to college, the most responsible and spiritual thing to do would be to save early for the eventual need. Investing can help you to achieve goals that the Lord has put on your heart that you otherwise may not be able to.

There are also several unbiblical reasons to invest. Unfortunately, these represent the greater number of investors, Christian and non-Christian, because Satan has so thoroughly dominated our attitudes about money.

Greed. Greed is the desire to continually have more and demand only the best.

"But those who want to get rich fall into temptation and a snare and many foolish and harmful desires which plunge men into ruin and destruction."

1 Timothy 6:9 NASB

Envy. Envy is the desire to achieve based on trying to have what others do.

"For I was envious of the arrogant, as I saw the prosperity of the wicked"

Psalm 73:3 NASB

Pride. Pride is the desire to be elevated because of material achievements.

"Instruct those who are rich in this present world not to be conceited or to fix their hope on the uncertainty of riches, but on God, who richly supplies us with all things to enjoy."

1 Timothy 6:17 NASB

Ignorance. Ignorance is following the counsel of other misguided people because of a lack of discernment.

"Leave the presence of a fool, or you will not discern words of knowledge."

Proverbs 14:7 NASB

There are many wrong motives for investing. The result of any of these is anxiety, frustration, and eventually a deadening of spiritual values. Thus, as our Lord says,

"No servant can serve two masters; for either he will hate the one, and love the other, or else he will be devoted to one, and despise the other. You cannot serve God and wealth."

Luke 16:13

How much should I invest?

Once you have accepted the purpose of investing (to serve God better), the crucial decision is how much to invest. Obviously, there is no absolute answer. It is an individual decision made after much prayer. With earnest prayer the decision is difficult—without it, impossible. There are some initial choices to be made that will greatly simplify the decision about how much to invest:

1. Before investing, give to God's work until you know that all of the needs God has placed on your heart are satisfied. Don't be misled into thinking that there will then be no

more needs in the world. There will always be needs, but God doesn't place every need on everyone's heart. Giving, like spiritual discernment, is a matter of growth and practice. I believe the key here is that when in doubt, give. It is better to be wrong and give too much than to ignore God's direction and give too little. The Spirit is never dampened by too sensitive a will, only by developing calluses.

"Therefore openly before the churches show them the proof of your love and of our reason for boasting about you."
2 Corinthians 8:24 NASB

2. Settle on a level of family needs that is God's plan for you. Too much spending on a family can rob surplus funds as surely as bad investments. Each Christian family must decide on the level God has planned for them and stick to it in spite of available surpluses. Remember that balance is essential. Too much is waste; too little is self-punishment.

3. Have a plan for the use of your potential surplus. One interesting characteristic about humans is that we can rationalize nearly anything, including reinvesting God's portion or saving it for Him. Therefore, it is important to settle on a plan for distributing the profits from investments before they arrive. Decide what portion is to be reinvested. Clearly, the greatest danger is to continually reinvest the

profits and rationalize it because of taxes, lack of discernable needs, or a need for surplus security. Do your planning before the money becomes available. One good way to do that is to give away a large percentage of the investment before it appreciates.

"Because of the proof given by this ministry they will glorify God for your obedience to your confession of the gospel of Christ, and for the liberality of your contribution to them and to all."

2 Corinthians 9:13 NASB

4. Remember,

"...Whatever we ask we receive from Him, because we keep His commandments and do the things that are pleasing in His sight."

1 John 3:22 NASB

PRACTICAL TOOLS

Buy affordable home

Shop around for lenders to get the best rate and to get a general idea of what lenders are offering. Once you choose to apply, they will need to run your credit score. Try to limit your application to only a few lenders. Every time there is a hard inquiry on your credit record, it lowers your credit score. Ask them and your realtor about all the fees that you will be charged. These can add up into the thousands, but if you are aware of them, you can often have the seller pay them or negotiate to lower them.

Be aware of the differences between a Fixed and ARM mortgage. Usually, a fixed mortgage is the better choice; however, there are a few situations (like if you plan to sell or refinance in one or two years) that an ARM mortgage may better suit your needs.

What about duration, such as 15-year, 30-year, and bi-monthly mortgages? There are many choices when it comes to the type of mortgages you can apply for. Research them all, and with the help of wise counsel, choose the one right for you.

Begin pre-paying your home mortgage

Make ownership of your home your first priority. Pay directly towards your principal on top of your regular monthly payments. Even $100 a month can save you thousands in interest over the life of your mortgage. Consider putting your bonuses and tax returns towards your mortgage after you have generously given from them.

Diversify investments

Investments should not change your lifestyle or cause stress or worry for you or your family. Don't allocate money for investing if your family budget doesn't allow for it. Remember that you are investing God's money. Always pray about your investments and ask yourself if they are a good use of God's resources.

Use strategies that provide safety and return:

- Seek wise counsel.
  - Don't be afraid to ask a person who you are considering hiring as an advisor for a list of references.
  - Make sure that you and your advisor have a similar risk tolerance factor.
  - Test your advisor's financial knowledge by asking them about a matter that you are very knowledgeable in.

- Diversification and good management
  - Before you invest, make a plan of how you will handle a surplus if you build one. This plan will keep you accountable to God with your investments.
  - Diversify your investments into at least 7 different sources.

- Investing for long-term
  - Investments gain over the long term, so you should have the ability to keep them in place before making the decision to invest.
  - Ensure that you are meeting with your planner or advisor on a regular basis to evaluate if you need to make adjustments.
  - Consider faith-based investments—i.e. Timothy based funds.

Increase giving to the Lord's work

Be sure that you have a plan for any windfall income. Know ahead of time what percent you want to spend on yourself, give to the Lord's work, or put aside for taxes.

Grow as a Steward

This Kingdom Investments chart is a visual way to examine how your personal investments stack up against your eternal ones. Make a note of how they compare, and write out a plan as to how you want to grow your Kingdom investments.

Categories	Short Term	Long Term	Total	Notes	
Major Purchases					Personal/Temporal Investments
Children's Education					
Retirement Fund					
Total					
Categories	International	National	Local	Total	Kingdom/Eternal Investments
Church					
Evangelism					
Discipleship					
The Poor					
Other					
Total					

Reward: What did you decide to do to reward yourself for completing this goal? Be sure you have written this down on your Money Map and here:

_____

_____

Devotional

Selecting the Right Counsel

"He who walks with the wise grows wise, but a companion of fools suffers harm."

Proverbs 13:20 NIV

If you're looking for an investment advisor, try to find someone who's a committed Christian.

Psalm 1:1 says we should avoid ungodly counsel. So, when you meet with a prospective advisor, test his or her value system. Advisors who will cheat for you will also cheat you. Advisors who will bend the rules on your behalf against someone else will do the same thing to you. If a person's counsel runs contrary to God's Word, discount it as worthless.

Proverbs 13:20 says we should look for wise counsel. You want someone who earns you more money than he or she costs you. When you first meet with an advisor, ask questions about a particular investment that you're knowledgeable about. Do research beforehand, if necessary. Then, if the advisor doesn't impress you with his or her answers, look elsewhere for advice.

Proverbs 15:22 says we are to have multiple counselors. Don't rely solely on the advice of one person. Ask trusted friends for their input. If you're married, seek the advice of your spouse. Finally, check a prospective advisor's references and ensure that he or she has integrity. Your spouse should have input into the selection of any prospective advisor. God may give sensitivity and discernment to one of you that the other does not have.

Chuck Bentley

Scripture Reading: Zechariah 1-6

Encouragement

I wanted a way to be able to increase my giving, and I did not know whether I should give one ministry a large donation, or spread my donation out among many ministries in smaller sums. I was pondering and praying, and I was put in contact with a Christian financial advisor who understood tithes and offerings. He proposed an idea—put the money into an investment and donate the dividends. I chose to that, and it has been so fun! I feel free to give as opportunities arise, and I have the funds available. I would not be able to otherwise do this as I am a single mother and a widow.

-Cecilia

My wife and I first encountered Crown through a seminar. Less than a year later, we co-led a small group study for about 12 weeks in our young marrieds class. We love being able to increase our giving to the Lord through this ministry! Also, because we had been prepaying our mortgage we were able to pay it off this year! By the grace of God we are debt free and can focus fully on providing for our son's and daughter's college expenses and continue planning for retirement. We are so happy to have more freedom to support the kingdom of God as He calls us to.

Tom and Lynn

Journal

_____

_____

_____

_____

_____

_____

_____

_____

_____

_____

Give a portion to seven, or even to eight, for you know not what disaster may happen on Earth.

Ecclesiastes 11:2 ESV

_____

_____

_____

_____

_____

_____

_____

_____

_____

_____

_____

It is not good to have zeal without knowledge, nor to be hasty and miss the way.

Proverbs 19:2 NIV

Do not lay up for yourselves treasures on earth, where moth and rust destroy and where thieves break in and steal, but lay up for yourselves treasures in heaven, where neither moth nor rust destroys and where thieves do not break in and steal.

Matthew 6:19-20 ESV

LEAVE A LEGACY

You will know the truth, and the truth will make you free.

JOHN 8:32 NASB

In this destination you will:

1. Evaluate your Kingdom impact for the next generation

2. Pay off home mortgage

3. Finalize children's education fund

4. Confirm estate plan is in order

5. Re-evaluate investments

6. Maximize generosity

DATE COMPLETED:_____

Many people in America seem to have a non-biblical view of retirement. It seems fundamentally wrong to seek to work two-thirds of our lives so that we can spend the final one-third on vacation.

The alternative course can be equally foolish. Others act as if they will remain young and highly employable for the rest of their lives. Often these people end up living on inadequate incomes, mostly Social Security, or being totally dependent on their children.

There are two fundamental points about retirement that you need to consider.

First, most Americans focus too much on ceasing work at too early an age.

Second, according to Proverbs 6:6-8, workers need to lay aside some surplus in higher-income-earning years so that the latter years can be spent in peace. "Go to the ant, O sluggard, observe her ways and be wise, which, having no chief, officer, or ruler, prepares her food in the summer and gathers her provision in the harvest" (NASB).

Your legacy

As you begin to think about preparing for your retirement and your estate, keep in mind that the most important thing you will leave to your family is not money or a home, it is their knowledge of your faith in Jesus Christ.

There are literally thousands of things to teach children about life—everything from how to tie a shoe to how to drive a car. There are academic lessons, culturally-appropriate manners, and infinitely more. In all your teaching, don't minimize the most important lesson of all: how to come to salvation in Jesus Christ.

Don't make the mistake of providing money, toys, vacations, nice homes, cars, and even college educations to your children and neglect the gift that will last eternally: a personal knowledge of Jesus Christ. Even if you're single or married without children, you can win people around you to Christ! You are a steward of your relationships.

PRACTICAL TOOLS

Evaluate your Kingdom impact for the next generation

There are many types of "legacies" one can leave behind—financial, spiritual, material, etc. Saint John Chrysostom said, "If you wish to leave much wealth to your children, leave them in God's care. Do not leave them riches, but virtue and skill." Here are some practical ways to invest now in order to leave a Kingdom-minded legacy that will impact generations to come.

Preparing Your Children

1. Place the children in your life high on your list of priorities, reserving an adequate portion of your time and energy to lead and train them.

2. Teach your children to pray for the Lord's guidance and provision. The Lord wants to demonstrate that He is actively involved in each of our lives. One way He does this is by answering our prayers. Because of our affluent society, we often rob ourselves of this opportunity. We can buy things or charge purchases without prayerfully allowing the Lord to supply them. We need to be creative in how we can

experience the reality of God in the area of our spending, and we need to be careful to communicate that value to our children.

3. Watch out for overindulgence. When it comes to money, parents are often on a tightrope trying to keep a healthy balance between being stingy and overindulgent.

4. Teach as you go. Though life today is extremely hectic, "teaching as you go" is a powerful way to instruct your children in the ways of the Lord, especially His financial principles.
   a. Show your children how much you are saving and why.
   b. Teach your children how costly debt is and how you've learned to pay off your debt.
   c. Let your children participate with you in the joy of giving!
   d. Show your children that you enjoy God's blessings with a thankful heart. Make it obvious!

5. Have your children shown faithfulness? Do your children have different financial needs? You do not have to leave the same amount to all of your children. Prayerfully consider how much should be left to each, and deeply consider discussing this with them before your passing.

6. Every financial decision you make is a valuable teaching opportunity. Obviously, the depth and substance of that

teaching will vary with the ages of your children, but this will always be true: "You're not fully preparing your children for life if you avoid teaching them biblical principles for handling their finances. And the earlier they learn, the better off they'll be!"

How Much Is Enough?

If your goal for the inheritance that you leave is simply for it to be as large as possible, you may want to take a moment to consider why you believe leaving a large sum is so important. This could ease some of your concerns if you lost money in an economic decline. If we can get beyond accumulation and preservation of money, we can be free to serve people and leave a much longer-lasting legacy.

The Bible certainly makes it clear that we are responsible for leaving a legacy. Proverbs 13:22 makes it clear that a good man thinks well beyond his own needs and makes plans for an inheritance that will extend to his grandchildren.

In spite of all the evidence that supports the fallacy that our children's primary need is money, we often fail to realize that an inheritance can and should be so much richer than the passing on of money and possessions to the next generation.

Instead, we should

- Leave a legacy of righteousness in the way you conduct your life
- Leave a legacy of love in the way you treat others
- Leave a legacy of faithfulness in the way that you love God
- Leave a legacy of joy in the way that you endure hardships
- Leave a legacy of generosity in the way you give
- Leave a legacy of character in the way you live out biblical values.

Follow the example of Christ: He left each of us with a model of an inheritance. He died on the cross to give us the true riches of a life with eternal security, eternal purpose and eternal treasures. His model frees us from self-absorption with the temporal, fleeting pursuit of earthly treasures. It gives us immense satisfaction of living a life in service to others as we look forward to "better and lasting possessions" (Hebrews 10:34 NIV). Leave your children and grandchildren an inheritance, one that will endure far longer than a deposit into their bank accounts.

Set short-range and long-range personal goals

Establish goals by weighing values as well as just setting objectives. Ask yourself, 'how much financial success is enough?' Monitoring your financial goals is critical because many Christians are trading their inheritance in eternity for a few temporary indulgences in this world. Few Christians understand the concept of eternal rewards, even though the Lord dedicated a great deal of His time on earth to teaching about them. The one certainty is that our position in the Lord's Kingdom will be inversely proportional to how we indulge ourselves in this life. "For those who exalt themselves will be humbled, and those who humble themselves will be exalted" (Matthew 23:12 NIV).

Take responsibility for your financial future and make the fundamental step of translating needs, wants, and desires into goals.

- Will you have financial resources to support your goals?
- Where do you want to be in 10, 20, 30 years?
- How do you handle unexpected emergencies or catastrophes?
- Are your records organized to the point your spouse or someone else can handle your affairs in case you become incapacitated?

Focus on following through with your plan, and achieve your goals.

- Pray to determine God's will concerning each goal.
- Write down your goals.
- Pray over your goals once they are in writing.
- File them in a safe place where they will not get lost.
- Refer to them and pray over them often to confirm and ensure that you are moving in the right direction.

Pay off home mortgage

As your finances are improving, considering paying your next month's principal. Refer to the amortization calculator. This can bring about significant savings in interest. Keep track of how much you have saved in interest to celebrate and encourage you to stay the course. Visit www.crown.org/my-mortgage

Remember to set up a home escrow account for taxes and insurance as your mortgage is being paid.

Do not be fooled, the tax write-off you receive for making mortgage payments does not have a greater advantage than simply paying the mortgage off in full. Pay your mortgage off as soon as you are able.

Finalize children's education fund

If the Lord has put it on your heart to send your child to college, do not rely on the government to pay for your child to go to school. Help your child to find ways to fully fund their degree, and consider helping them through an education savings fund.

Discourage your children from borrowing for student loans. If your student is planning on taking out loans, have them create a plan before going to college for how that money should be spent. Help your child to estimate what their monthly payments will be after they graduate to show them the danger of taking out large loans.

Fully examine all higher learning opportunities, including online courses, joining the military, community colleges, and colleges close to home.

Research scholarship funds with your child and encourage them to apply for as many possible. There are thousands of opportunities for scholarships from colleges, businesses, community organizations, etc. Encourage your children to participate in paying for their education.

Confirm estate plan is in order

Research the difference between a will and a revocable living trust and determine which is right for you.

As you organize your estate, keep all of your information organized so that anyone can easily understand it. Take time to make any decisions you need to concerning living wills, health directive, power of attorney, pour-over will, etc. There are many facets of estate planning. For example, did you know that you can add beneficiaries or co-owners on your accounts even without a will? You will likely want to seek wise counsel to help you create a qualified estate plan.

Giving from your estate is an excellent way to be a good steward, even after your passing. Consider which groups, such as your church or a nonprofit, you would like to give to, and inquire as to the best way to do so.

Re-evaluate investments

As you continue investing, be sure that have taken inflation into account. Earning too little on your investments is one of the greatest obstacles to investment success. It's not enough to just preserve what you have now. It's impossible to know exactly what rates inflation will take on, but you can start by assuming that it will at least mirror the past. Your monthly income will need to grow every year in order to keep the same purchasing power. Let's say that you believe you can comfortably live on $4,000 a month in your retirement. Assuming 3% inflation, in 30 years your $4,000 per month would need to be $9,827 per month. Be sure to diversify your investments between low-risk opportunities and opportunities that will offer you a greater return.

You might also want to consider adopting the dollar cost averaging technique. Set aside an amount each month to invest in a mutual fund or to buy shares of stock in a particular company. Each investment you made in the mutual fund would buy a certain number of shares in the fund, depending on what the share price was at that particular time. Both the share prices for stocks and mutual funds would fluctuate. This method encourages consistency which is important if you want the best return on your investment dollar.

Maximize generosity

Giving should be a key priority. "Honor the Lord with your wealth and with the firstfruits of all your produce" (Proverbs 3:9 ESV). As soon as we receive income, we should set aside the amount we are to give. This habit helps us to keep Christ first in all we do and defeats the temptation to spend what we have set aside for giving.

Give prayerfully, exercising the same care as when we decide where to work, save, or invest. Also give without pride. Matthew 6:1-4, "Beware of practicing your righteousness before other people in order to be seen by them, for then you will have no reward from your Father who is in heaven. Thus, when you give to the needy, sound no trumpet before you, as the hypocrites do in the synagogues and in the streets, that they may be praised by others. Truly, I say to you, they have received their reward. But when you give to the needy, do not let your left hand know what your right hand is doing, so that your giving may be in secret. And your Father who sees in secret will reward you" (ESV). To experience God's blessing and joy, never give to impress people.

Giving should also be personal. "Each one of you should." It's the responsibility of every child of God to give. The advantages of giving are intended for each person, and each one must participate to enjoy the blessing of generosity.

Grow as a Steward

Think about your children or young people who you see on a regular basis to whom you could offer discipleship. The spiritual legacy which you will leave behind is greater than any monetary legacy that you could imagine.

List four practical lessons you will teach them to help them become faithful with money and possessions.

1. _____

2. _____

3. _____

4. _____

Reward: What did you decide to do to reward yourself for completing this goal? Be sure you have written this down on your Money Map and here:

_____

_____

Devotional

Reflection

As I look back over the years, I have a few regrets; one, that I was not saved at a younger age so I would have had longer to serve the Lord. Two, that I didn't know more while my children were at home so I could have spent more time teaching them God's ways.

Obviously I can't do anything about the past, so I'm trying to pass along what I know to my grandchildren.

Other than those, I have no conscious regrets. For decades, God has allowed me to do exactly what He called me to do; I've never done anything in my life that I have enjoyed more. Of course, there were some parts I didn't enjoy, but that's true with anything, isn't it?

It is unfortunate that so few people can look back over their lives with few regrets. It's a good idea to examine this past year, to see if there's anything you regret. You can correct it right now. It's never too late. Make up your mind that next year will be different.

We will all face judgment one day and should be prepared. You can't do anything about the past, but you don't have to continually live in it either.

"We will all stand before the judgment seat of God."

Romans 14:10 NASB

Larry Burkett

Scripture Reading: Numbers 6:60

Encouragement

After I began studying from Crown, I wasn't content to just sit on the principles I'd learned. I wanted to teach them to my children. I recognized an important truth: stewardship begins in the home. It's the place where we have the greatest opportunity to influence the next generation. I gave each of my children one of Crown's youth studies. A few weeks into the study, all three children became very involved in the learning process. It became fun; it was about them and the Lord, not about Dad trying to be cheap. They could have gone into the studies kicking and screaming or with quiet resistance. But it wasn't a stretch for them to participate. The principles become a part of who you are. This is what I wanted for my children. I wanted them to do what was right when no one was watching, and this is especially true for that day when they leave home to go to college and live on their own. What has happened in our family is amazing, but it's not because we're anything special, but because when we stand before the Lord, we'll have something worthwhile to give Him because we followed His financial principles.

-The Schafer Family

Sometimes it gets overwhelming when I think about this recession and financial attitude of our nation and leaders, and I feel helpless as to what an at-home mom can do.

Then the Lord speaks to me in a still small voice and says, "You are making a difference. You are teaching your sons my principles, you are following my principles, and you are facilitating my principles through Crown by teaching the Bible study. Teach it again." OK, Lord!

In the last 2 years we have taken a 40% cut in pay but, because of God's principles, we are doing fine. The Lord has chosen to bless my husband's cabinet/furniture making business recently, and we have lots of work lined up. Praise God!

-Hank and Lydia

Journal

By wisdom a house is built, and by understanding it is established; and by knowledge the rooms are filled with all precious and pleasant riches.

Proverbs 24:3-4 NASB

_____

_____

_____

_____

_____

_____

_____

_____

_____

_____

Whoever brings blessing will be enriched, and one who waters will himself be watered.

Proverbs 11:25 ESV

_____

_____

_____

_____

_____

_____

_____

_____

_____

_____

In all things I have shown you that by working hard in this way we must help the weak and remember the words of the Lord Jesus, how he himself said, "It is more blessed to give than to receive."

Acts 20:35 ESV

_____

_____

_____

_____

_____

_____

_____

_____

_____

_____

You were bought with a price; do not become bondservants of men.

1 Corinthians 7:23 ESV

MONEY AND POSSESSION

SCRIPTURES

GOD'S PART

Genesis 14:19	Ezra 6:22
Genesis 14:22	Nehemiah 2:8, 18
Exodus 9:29	Exodus 3:21-22
Exodus 19:5	Exodus 12:35-36
Deuteronomy 10:14	Exodus 14:4
1 Chronicles 29:11,14-16	Deuteronomy 2:30
Job 41:11	Exodus 34:23-24
Psalm 24:1	Acts 17:26
Psalm 50:12	2 Chronicles 25:7-9
Psalm 82:8	Isaiah 10:5-6
Psalm 89:11	1 Chronicles 29:14
Psalm 95:4-5	Romans 11:36
Psalm 104:24	Genesis 22:14
1 Corinthians 10:26	Psalm 136:25
Matthew 25:14-28	Psalm 145:15-16
Hebrews 1:3	Deuteronomy 2:7
Colossians 1:17	Deuteronomy 8:15-16
Leviticus 25:23	Nehemiah 9:15
Ezekiel 16:17	Nehemiah 9:21
Haggai 2:8	Leviticus 25:20-22
Psalm 50:10-11	Matthew 14:15-21
1 Chronicles 29:11-12	Matthew 15:32-38
Psalm 135:6	Matthew 16:8-10
Proverbs 16:33	Mark 6:35-44
Proverbs 20:24	Mark 8:1-9
Daniel 2:20-21	Mark 8:18-20
Job 42:11	Luke 9:12-17
Isaiah 45:6-7	John 6:5-13
Lamentations 3:37-38	John 21:2-11
Amos 3:6	Psalm 33:18-19
Romans 8:28	Psalm 34:9-10
Genesis 45:5-9	Psalm 81:13,16
Ecclesiastes 9:11	Proverbs 10:3
Proverbs 21:1	Philippians 4:19
Genesis 39:21	Matthew 6:33

Luke 12:30-31	Psalm 66:10-12
1 Chronicles 29:14	Psalm 127:2
Romans 11:36	Proverbs 10:22
1 Timothy 6:17	2 Samuel 12:7-8
1 Chronicles 29:12,14-16	Matthew 25:14-15
Ecclesiastes 5:19	Genesis 32:9
Ecclesiastes 6:1-2	Genesis 32:12
Jeremiah 27:5	Genesis 39:2-3
Genesis 35:12	Genesis 39:21-23
Exodus 6:8	Psalm 115:14
Leviticus 25:38	Psalm 118:25
Deuteronomy 6:10-12	3 John 2
Deuteronomy 8:7-10	Job 1:21-22
Deuteronomy 26:1-3	Job 2:9-10
Joshua 24:13	1 Samuel 2:7
Nehemiah 9:15	Ecclesiastes 7:14
Nehemiah 9:36	Judges 2:13-16
Jeremiah 7:5-7	Jeremiah 29:14
Genesis 24:35	Jeremiah 32:44
Genesis 26:12-14	Jeremiah 33:7, 11, 26
Deuteronomy 30:5	Jeremiah 48:47
1 Samuel 18:14-15	Jeremiah 49:6
2 Samuel 6:12	Joel 3:1-2
2 Chronicles 1:11-12	Zephaniah 2:7
2 Chronicles 25:6-9	Zephaniah 3:20
Job 1:9-10	Zechariah 8:10-12
Job 42:10,12	Proverbs 15:25
Psalm 105:37	Ezekiel 26:12, 14
Isaiah 45:3	Zechariah 9:3-4
Jeremiah 27:5-7	Zechariah 14:1-2
Ezekiel 16:13,14,17-19	Genesis 31:6-7, 9
Ezekiel 29:18-19	Genesis 31:14-16
Hosea 2:8	Job 1:9-10
Genesis 14:22-23	Genesis 31:42
Deuteronomy 8:15-18	

OUR PART

Genesis 1:28
Psalm 8:6
Psalm 115:16
Hebrews 2:6-8
Matthew 25:14
Genesis 24:2
Genesis 39:4-6
Genesis 39:7-9
1 Corinthians 9:17
Luke 14:33
Matthew 19:27-29
Mark 10:28-30
Luke 18:28-30
Mark 1:20
Luke 5:11
Luke 5:27-28
Matthew 13:44-46
1 Corinthians 4:2, KJV Proverbs 28:20
Matthew 24:44-46
Matthew 25:21
Matthew 25:20-23
Luke 12:42-44
Luke 19:12-26
Matthew 24:48-51
Luke 12:45-47
Luke 19:12-26
Luke 16:1-8
Deuteronomy 7:12-13
Deuteronomy 15:4-6
Deuteronomy 28:1-14
Deuteronomy 29:9
Deuteronomy 30:9-10
Deuteronomy 30:15-16
Joshua 1:8

1 Kings 2:3
1 Chronicles 22:12-13
1 Chronicles 28:8
Psalm 37:4
Psalm 128:1-2
2 Kings 18:6-7
2 Chronicles 14:7
2 Chronicles 26:5
2 Chronicles 31:20-21
Isaiah 30:22-23
Deuteronomy 28:15-18, 33
Deuteronomy 28:45-48, 63
Deuteronomy 30:15-18
Ezra 7:26
Judges 2:13-14
2 Chronicles 21:12-14,16,17
2 Chronicles 24:20
Nehemiah 9:33-36
Jeremiah 10:21
Ezekiel 16:17-19, 39
Haggai 1:4-11
Haggai 2:15-17
Psalm 112:1,3
Proverbs 22:4
Proverbs 28:25
Proverbs 11:28
Jeremiah 17:5-6
Jeremiah 48:7
Jeremiah 49:4-5
Matthew 25:14, 19
Luke 16:2
2 Corinthians 5:9-10
Revelation 20:11-12

DEBT

Romans 13:8
Proverbs 22:7
1 Corinthians 7:23
1 Samuel 22:1-2
2 Kings 4:1
Nehemiah 5:1-5
Psalm 109:11
Isaiah 50:1
Jeremiah 15:10
Deuteronomy 28:15, 43-45
Deuteronomy 15:4-6
Deuteronomy 28:1-2, 12
Proverbs 3:27-28
Psalm 37:21

2 Kings 4:1-7
Deuteronomy 15:1-11
Deuteronomy 31:10-11
Nehemiah 10:31
Philemon 18-19
Matthew 18:21-35
Luke 7:40-43
Colossians 2:14
Proverbs 17:18
Proverbs 20:16
Proverbs 27:13
Proverbs 11:15
Proverbs 22:26-27
Proverbs 6:1-5

COUNSEL

Proverbs 1:5
Proverbs 1:25
Proverbs 1:30
Proverbs 12:15
Proverbs 13:10
Proverbs 19:20
Proverbs 20:18
Proverbs 27:9
Ecclesiastes 4:13
Luke 13:31
Proverbs 11:14
Proverbs 15:22
Proverbs 24:5-6
Leviticus 26:8
Ecclesiastes 4:9-12
Exodus 18:14-24
1 Kings 1:11-12

Job 29:21-23
2 Chronicles 25:14-16
Job 12:13
Psalm 16:7
Psalm 25:12
Psalm 32:8
Psalm 33:10-11
Psalm 73:24
Proverbs 19:21
Isaiah 9:6
Isaiah 11:2
Isaiah 28:29
Jeremiah 32:18-19
1 Chronicles 10:13-14
Joshua 9:14-15
Psalm 106:13-15
Psalm 107:10-12

2 Samuel 15:31, 33-34
2 Samuel 16:20, 23
2 Samuel 17:6-23
Psalm 119:24
Proverbs 1:8-9
Proverbs 6:20-22
Proverbs 23:22
1 Kings 2:1-4
2 Chronicles 9:23
Proverbs 13:20
1 Corinthians 12:8
1 Kings 12:6-8
2 Chronicles 10:6-8
Job 21:14-16
Psalm 1:1
Proverbs 12:5
Ezra 4:4-5
Nahum 1:11
Deuteronomy 32:28
Isaiah 41:28-29
1 Kings 12:8-10, 13-14

2 Chronicles 10:8-10, 13-14
Proverbs 11:14
Proverbs 15:22
Proverbs 24:6
Psalm 32:8
Psalm 73:24
Proverbs 6:20-22
Proverbs 13:10
Proverbs 19:20
Proverbs 12:20
1 Chronicles 10:13,14
2 Chronicles 22:3-5
2 Chronicles 25:16
Proverbs 1:24-32
Proverbs 13:10
Proverbs 15:22
Proverbs 11:14
Joshua 9:14-15
Psalm 106:13-15
Psalm 107:10-12

HONESTY

Genesis 8:21
Jeremiah 17:9
Matthew 15:19
Mark 7:21-22
Judges 17:6
Genesis 31:7
Joshua 7:11, 20-21
1 Samuel 8:3
1 Kings 21:19
Psalm 58:3
Isaiah 1:23
Isaiah 56:11

Jeremiah 6:13
Jeremiah 7:9, 11
Ezekiel 22:27, 29
Hosea 4:1-2
Hosea 5:10
Hosea 7:1
Hosea 12:7
Micah 6:10-12
John 12:4-6
John 18:40
Acts 5:1-10
Titus 1:12

Revelation 9:20-21	Proverbs 22:22-23
Luke 16:1-8	Proverbs 22:28
Jeremiah 7:9-11	Proverbs 23:10
Matthew 21:12-13	Proverbs 23:23
Matthew 23:25	Proverbs 28:24
Mark 11:15-17	Lamentations 3:35-36
Luke 11:39	Zechariah 8:16-17
Luke 19:45-46	Luke 3:12-14
Titus 1:10-11	Romans 2:21-22
John 1:14	1 Corinthians 6:7-10
John 14:6	Ephesians 4:25
John 16:13	Ephesians 6:14
1 John 5:7	Colossians 3:9
John 8:44	1 Thessalonians 5:22
Exodus 20:15	1 Timothy 1:9-10
Leviticus 19:11-13	Titus 2:9-10
Leviticus 19:35-36	1 Peter 1:15-16
Leviticus 25:14-17	1 Peter 4:15
Deuteronomy 5:19	Exodus 18:21-22
Deuteronomy 19:14	Proverbs 20:28
Deuteronomy 25:13-16	Proverbs 28:16
Psalm 34:13	Ezekiel 45:9-10
Psalm 51:6	1 Timothy 3:8
Psalm 62:10	Titus 1:7
Proverbs 3:3	1 Peter 5:1-2
Proverbs 4:24	Malachi 1:13-14
Proverbs 6:12	Malachi 3:8-9
Proverbs 6:16, 19	Proverbs 19:1
Proverbs 11:1	Proverbs 19:22
Proverbs 12:22	Proverbs 28:12
Proverbs 13:5	Numbers 16:15
Proverbs 14:5	1 Samuel 12:3-5
Proverbs 14:25	Job 31:5, 8
Proverbs 17:7	Daniel 6:4
Proverbs 16:11	Daniel 6:22
Proverbs 20:10	Zephaniah 3:13
Proverbs 20:23	Genesis 42:11, 18-20

Genesis 42:31-34
Proverbs 13:5
Proverbs 14:2
Proverbs 26:28
Romans 13:9-10
Philippians 2:15
Proverbs 4:24-26
Luke 16:10
Psalm 119:36
Proverbs 30:7-8
Galatians 5:16-17
Matthew 7:12
Philippians 2:4
Proverbs 16:6
Psalm 26:4
Psalm 40:4
Psalm 101:6-7
Proverbs 1:10-16
Proverbs 29:24
1 Corinthians 5:9-11
1 Corinthians 15:33
Ephesians 4:28
Genesis 30:31-33
Leviticus 5:5-6
Leviticus 6:1-5, 7
1 John 1:9
Proverbs 28:13
James 5:16
Exodus 22:1-4
Exodus 22:7-9
Exodus 22:14
Leviticus 6:1-5
Numbers 5:5-8
2 Samuel 12:5-6
Proverbs 6:30-31
Ezekiel 33:14-16
Luke 19:8

Psalm 15:1-4
Psalm 24:3-4
Psalm 145:18
Proverbs 3:3-4
Proverbs 3:32
Proverbs 12:22
Jeremiah 22:15-17
Proverbs 2:7
Proverbs 10:9
Isaiah 33:15-16
Proverbs 20:7
Proverbs 10:2
Deuteronomy 25:13-15
Psalm 34:12-13
Proverbs 12:19
Ezekiel 33:14-16
Proverbs 3:3-4
Proverbs 15:6
Proverbs 28:16
Deuteronomy 25:13-16
Psalm 5:6
Proverbs 3:32
Proverbs 6:16, 19
Proverbs 12:22
Proverbs 19:9
Isaiah 57:17
Isaiah 59:2-4
Deuteronomy 27:17
Psalm 63:11
Proverbs 12-15
Proverbs 19:5
Proverbs 20:17
Isaiah 57:17
Jeremiah 5:27-29
Jeremiah 9:3-9
Ezekiel 22:13-15
Ezekiel 22:27-31

Hosea 5:10

Amos 8:4-10

Micah 6:10-16

Matthew 21:12-13 ·

Luke 19:45-46

Joshua 7:11, 15, 25

Psalm 5:6

Psalm 52:3-5

Proverbs 1:19

Proverbs 6:12, 15

Proverbs 12:19

Proverbs 21:6

Proverbs 22:8

Proverbs 22:22-23

Jeremiah 22:17-19

Ezekiel 18:10-13, 18

Acts 5:1-10

Proverbs 15:27

Jeremiah 8:10

Micah 2:1-3

Genesis 31:7, 9

Proverbs 10:2

Proverbs 13:11

Jeremiah 6:12-13

Jeremiah 17:11

Micah 4:13

Proverbs 22:8

Proverbs 29:12

Revelation 21:8

Revelation 21:27

Revelation 22:15

Deuteronomy 27:17

Proverbs 20:17

Nahum 3:1

Job 24:1-2, 12

Proverbs 17:8

Proverbs 21:14

Psalm 26:9-10

Proverbs 17:23

1 Samuel 8:3

Isaiah 1:23

Micah 7:3

Matthew 28:11-15

Acts 24:25-26

Exodus 23:8

Deuteronomy 16:19

Ecclesiastes 7:7

Deuteronomy 10:17

2 Chronicles 19:7

Proverbs 29:4

1 Samuel 12:3-5

Job 6:22

Deuteronomy 27:25

Isaiah 5:23

Ezekiel 22:12-15

Amos 5:11-12

Micah 3:11-12

Psalm 15:1, 5

Proverbs 15:27

Isaiah 33:15-16

GIVING

James 2:14-17

1 John 3:17

2 Corinthians 8:8

Luke 10:33-35

Matthew 19:21-22

Mark 10:21-22

Luke 18:22-23

John 3:16

1 John 4:16

James 1:17

1 Corinthians 13:3

2 Corinthians 9:7

Exodus 25:2

Exodus 30:12-14

Exodus 35:5

Exodus 35:21-29

Leviticus 7:14

Numbers 18:8-24

2 Chronicles 32:23

1 Chronicles 18:11

2 Samuel 8:11

Psalm 50:14

Psalm 66:13

Psalm 68:29

Psalm 76:11

Ezekiel 20:40

Micah 4:13

1 Chronicles 29:14-16

Matthew 2:1

Isaiah 43:23-24

1 Chronicles 29:5-9

1 Chronicles 29:14-17

2 Corinthians 8:1-5

Matthew 23:23

Luke 11:42

Luke 18:10-14

Genesis 4:4

Hebrews 11:4

Philippians 4:18

Genesis 4:3-5

Amos 4:4-6

Amos 5:22, 24

Amos 5:25-27

Malachi 2:13-14

Acts 5:1-10

Proverbs 7:14

Acts 20:35

Matthew 6:21

Luke 12:34

Matthew 6:20

Matthew 19:21

Luke 12:33

Luke 18:22

Philippians 4:17

1 Timothy 6:17-19

Deuteronomy 14:28-29

2 Chronicles 31:10

Proverbs 3:9-10

Proverbs 11:24-25

Ecclesiastes 11:1

Luke 6:38

2 Corinthians 9:6-11

Philippians 4:19

Malachi 3:10

Ezekiel 44:30

Luke 7:2-5

Acts 9:36-37, 40

Acts 10:1-4, 31

Genesis 14:20

Genesis 28:20-22

Leviticus 27:30-32

Malachi 3:8-9

Deuteronomy 14:22-26

Numbers 18:21-24

Deuteronomy 14:28-29

Deuteronomy 26:12

2 Chronicles 31:4-12

Nehemiah 10:37-38

Nehemiah 13:10-11

Numbers 18:26

Hebrews 7:1-2, 4-9

2 Chronicles 31:11-12

Nehemiah 10:38

Nehemiah 12:44

Nehemiah 13:12

Deuteronomy 16:10, 16

1 Corinthians 16:2

Ezra 2:69

Acts 11:29

2 Corinthians 8:12

Mark 12:41-44

Luke 21:1-4

2 Corinthians 8:1-4

2 Samuel 24:21-24

1 Chronicles 21:22-24

Malachi 1:6-14

Exodus 23:10-11

Exodus 34:19

Exodus 34:26

Leviticus 2:12

Numbers 28:26

Deuteronomy 26:1-2

Proverbs 3:9

Exodus 22:29

Deuteronomy 23:21

Ecclesiastes 5:4

2 Corinthians 9:7

1 Corinthians 16:2

Exodus 34:20

Deuteronomy 16:17

Ezekiel 45:16

Acts 11:29

1 Corinthians 16:2

1 Corinthians 16:2

Matthew 6:1-4

Exodus 25:2

Exodus 35:5

Exodus 35:21-29

2 Kings 12:4

1 Chronicles 26:20

1 Chronicles 26:26

2 Chronicles 31:14-15

Nehemiah 12:44

Nehemiah 13:13

2 Corinthians 8:18-21

Acts 11:30

1 Corinthians 16:3-4

2 Kings 12:15

2 Kings 22:7

1 Timothy 5:8

Matthew 15:4-6

Mark 7:9-13

1 Timothy 5:4

1 Timothy 5:16

Genesis 45:11

Genesis 47:12

Leviticus 2:3

Leviticus 7:14

Leviticus 7:32-34

Leviticus 10:12-14

Numbers 5:8-10

Numbers 18:8-19

Numbers 31:28-30

Deuteronomy 18:3-4

Deuteronomy 25:4

Nehemiah 10:35-36

Nehemiah 12:47

Ezekiel 44:29-30

Matthew 10:9-10

Mark 6:8

Luke 9:1-3

Luke 10:1, 4-7

Galatians 6:6

1 Timothy 5:17-18

Titus 3:13	Ezekiel 16:49
3 John 1:5-8	Exodus 23:10-11
Luke 8:3	Leviticus 19:9-10
1 Corinthians 9:6-15	Leviticus 23:22
1 Corinthians 9:17-18	Deuteronomy 24:19-21
2 Corinthians 11:7-9	Deuteronomy 15:7-10
2 Corinthians 12:14-18	Ester 9:22
1 Thessalonians 2:5, 9	Leviticus 25:10
2 Thessalonians 3:8-9	Job 29:12-16
1 Peter 5:1-2	Job 31:16-23
2 Corinthians 2:17	Psalm 72:4, 12-13
Titus 1:10-11	Proverbs 31:10, 20
2 Peter 2:1, 3	Luke 3:10-11
Luke 22:35-36	Matthew 25:31-45
Exodus 25:3-8	John 13:27-29
Exodus 36:3-7	Ephesians 4:28
1 Chronicles 29:2-8	Acts 2:44-45
1 Kings 5:17	Acts 11:28-30
2 Kings 12:4-11	Acts 20:35
2 Kings 22:4-6	Romans 15:26-27
2 Chronicles 24:4-13	Galatians 2:10
2 Chronicles 34:8-11	Jeremiah 22:16
Ezra 2:68-69	Ezekiel 18:7, 9, 16-17
Ezra 6:4	Psalm 112:2, 9
Ezra 6:8	Proverbs 28:27
Nehemiah 10:30, 39	Psalm 41:1-3
Matthew 5:42	Psalm 41:1-2
Luke 6:30	Psalm 112:9
Galatians 6:10	Deuteronomy 15:10
Romans 12:10, 13	Deuteronomy 24:19
Proverbs 25:21-22	Psalm 72:4, 12-15
Romans 12:20	Psalm 112:3, 9
Proverbs 28:17	Proverbs 19:17
Deuteronomy 15:11	Proverbs 28:8
Proverbs 14:31	Daniel 4:27
Proverbs 19:17	Titus 3:13-14
Isaiah 58:6-10	Proverbs 22:9

Proverbs 14:21

Proverbs 21:13

Proverbs 22:16

Proverbs 28:27

Job 30:25

Job 29:16

Job 22:5, 7, 9

Matthew 26:6-13

Mark 14:3-7

John 12:3-8

Acts 6:1-3

James 1:27

Acts 4:32-33

Leviticus 5:7, 11

Leviticus 12:6, 8

Leviticus 14:21-22

Leviticus 14:30-32

Leviticus 27:8

Luke 2:22-24

Exodus 30:12-15

Luke 19:8-9

Genesis 24:22, 53

Genesis 43:11-12, 15

2 Chronicles 9:8-9

2 Chronicles 9:12

2 Chronicles 31:23

2 Chronicles 32:23

2 Chronicles 35:7-9

Ezra 1:4, 6

Nehemiah 7:70-72

Esther 2:18

Psalm 72:10

Jeremiah 40:5

Genesis 32:13, 20

Genesis 33:8-11

Proverbs 21:14

Genesis 34:11-12

2 Chronicles 9:23-24

1 Kings 10:10

Revelation 11:10

Exodus 23:19

Exodus 34:26

Deuteronomy 12:6

Deuteronomy 12:11

Deuteronomy 12:17-18

Acts 3:2-6

Proverbs 19:6

2 Corinthians 9:5

2 Corinthians 9:12

Matthew 5:23-24

Nahum 1:15

Hebrews 13:16

Matthew 8:4

Mark 1:44

Luke 5:14

Acts 24:17

Mark 12:33

Hosea 6:6

1 Samuel 15:22

Isaiah 1:11

Proverbs 21:3

Ezekiel 46:11-15

Ezekiel 46:12

1 Kings 8:62-64

Ezra 1:2, 4, 6

Ezra 7:15-18, 20-22

Romans 12:6-8

Exodus 16:18

2 Corinthians 8:13-15

WORK

Genesis 2:2-3	Luke 19:2
John 5:17	Acts 16:14
Exodus 20:9	1 Corinthians 10:31
Exodus 23:12	Ephesians 6:5-9
Exodus 34:21	Colossians 3:17
Deuteronomy 5:13	Colossians 3:23-24
Ephesians 4:28	Ecclesiastes 1:3
2 Thessalonians 3:8-12	Ecclesiastes 2:4-5, 10-11
Psalm 104:23	Ecclesiastes 2:18-24
Genesis 2:15	Ecclesiastes 3:9-10, 13
Genesis 3:17-19, 23	Ecclesiastes 4:4-6
Genesis 5:29	Ecclesiastes 5:18-19
Genesis 2:15	Ecclesiastes 6:7
Genesis 4:2	1 Samuel 2:28
Genesis 9:20	Psalm 90:17
Genesis 46:32	John 4:34
Genesis 47:3	John 6:27
Amos 7:14	Acts 13:36
Genesis 39:4	1 Corinthians 3:13-15
Genesis 41:41	Ephesians 2:10
Genesis 45:26	John 17:4
Nehemiah 4:14	John 21:3-11
Psalm 105:21	Psalm 127:1
Daniel 2:48	Proverbs 16:3
Daniel 6:1-2	Romans 2:6, 8
Daniel 8:27	2 Corinthians 5:9-10
Acts 8:27	James 3:14-16
Matthew 4:18	Jeremiah 45:5
Mark 1:16	Joshua 1:6-7
Mark 1:20	1 Chronicles 22:10, 13, 16
Matthew 13:55	1 Chronicles 28:20
Mark 6:3	2 Chronicles 15:7
Acts 18:2-3	Haggai 2:4
Mark 2:14	Ezra 4:4-5
Luke 5:27	Nehemiah 4:15-22

Nehemiah 6:3, 9	Proverbs 6:9-11
Proverbs 12:27	Proverbs 10:4
Ecclesiastes 9:10	Proverbs 14:23
Ecclesiastes 11:6	Proverbs 20:13
Genesis 31:38-40	Proverbs 23:21
Nehemiah 2:18	Proverbs 24:30-34
Acts 20:34	Ecclesiastes 10:18
1 Corinthians 4:11-12	Proverbs 21:25
2 Corinthians 11:27	Proverbs 13:4
Colossians 1:29	Proverbs 12:24
1 Thessalonians 2:9	Genesis 2:2-3
2 Thessalonians 3:8	Exodus 20:11
Proverbs 16:26	Exodus 31:17
2 Timothy 2:6	Hebrews 4:4, 10
Proverbs 12:11	Exodus 12:16
Proverbs 27:18	Exodus 20:9-10
Proverbs 28:19	Exodus 23:12
Proverbs 10:4-5	Exodus 34:21
Proverbs 13:11	Leviticus 23:3
Proverbs 14:23	Deuteronomy 5:13-14
Proverbs 21:5	Nehemiah 10:31
Proverbs 13:4	Jeremiah 17:21-22, 24
Proverbs 12:24	Exodus 31:15
Ecclesiastes 5:12	Numbers 15:32-35
Psalm 128:1-2	Nehemiah 13:15-18
Psalm 127:2	Jeremiah 7:27
Proverbs 23:4	Exodus 23:10-11
Proverbs 6:6-8	Leviticus 25:1-5
Proverbs 10:26	Nehemiah 10:31
Proverbs 12:27	Leviticus 26:34
Proverbs 15:19	Leviticus 26:43
Proverbs 18:9	Leviticus 25:11
Proverbs 19:24	Numbers 28:18
Proverbs 22:13	Numbers 28:25
Proverbs 26:13-16	Deuteronomy 16:8
Proverbs 19:15	Leviticus 16:29
Proverbs 20:4	Leviticus 23:27-31

Leviticus 23:7-8
Leviticus 23:34-36
Numbers 29:12, 35
Leviticus 23:21
Leviticus 23:24-25
Numbers 28:26
Numbers 29:1
Numbers 29:7
Exodus 28:3
Exodus 31:1-3
Exodus 31:6
Exodus 35:30-35
Exodus 36:1-2
1 Chronicles 22:12
2 Chronicles 1:11-12
2 Chronicles 9:23
Ecclesiastes 2:26
Daniel 1:17
Daniel 2:21, 23
Genesis 39:2-3
Ruth 2:12
1 Chronicles 22:11
Nehemiah 2:18, 20
Nehemiah 4:15, 19-20
Nehemiah 6:15-16
John 3:27
1 Chronicles 29:12
2 Chronicles 9:8
Psalm 75:6-7
Daniel 2:37-38
Daniel 5:21
Haggai 1:14
Jeremiah 22:13
Malachi 3:5
Genesis 29:15
Genesis 30:28
James 5:1, 3-4

Matthew 20:1-16
Leviticus 19:13
Deuteronomy 24:14-15
Colossians 4:1
Ephesians 6:7-9
Job 31:13-15
Isaiah 58:3
Proverbs 29:12
Exodus 21:2
Deuteronomy 15:12-14
Genesis 30:27
Genesis 39:5
Nehemiah 5:14-18
Exodus 1:13-14
Proverbs 26:10
Daniel 6:4
1 Timothy 6:2
Proverbs 17:2
Proverbs 27:18
Daniel 6:28
2 Kings 12:15
2 Kings 22:7
2 Chronicles 34:12
Proverbs 25:13
Ephesians 6:5-8
Colossians 3:22-24
Titus 2:9-10
1 Peter 2:18-19
1 Timothy 6:1
Titus 2:9
Proverbs 30:10
Luke 3:14
Genesis 39:7-9
2 Corinthians 6:14-17
Proverbs 24:27
Proverbs 14:4
Proverbs 22:29

James 4:13-15	1 Kings 9:10-12
1 Thessalonians 4:11-12	Number 8:24-26
Acts 19:24-28	Proverbs 31:10-28
Psalm 107:11-12	Titus 2:4-5
1 Kings 5:6	Proverbs 12:11
2 Chronicles 2:9-10	Proverbs 28:19

SAVING AND INVESTING

Matthew 6:19-21	Genesis 48:21-22
Matthew 6:24-33	Joshua 24:32
Matthew 19:16-21	Ruth 4:5-10
Mark 6:8	2 Chronicles 21:3
Luke 5:11	Ecclesiastes 5:13-14
Luke 12:22-34	Ecclesiastes 7:11
Luke 18:18-30	1 Chronicles 28:8
Luke 12:13-21	Ezra 9:12
Matthew 25:14-28	Psalm 25:12-13
Luke 19:12-24	Proverbs 17:2
1 Timothy 5:8	Luke 15:11-31
Proverbs 13:22	Luke 12:13-15
Proverbs 19:14	Proverbs 20:21
Isaiah 38:1	Galatians 4:1-2
2 Corinthians 12:14	Ecclesiastes 2:18-21
Leviticus 25:46	Ecclesiastes 4:8
Numbers 27:8-11	1 Timothy 6:9
Numbers 36:2-9	1 Timothy 6:10
Deuteronomy 18:8	1 Timothy 6:11
Deuteronomy 21:15-17	Matthew 4:8-10
Ezekiel 46:16-18	Luke 4:5-8
Numbers 18:20-24	Proverbs 21:20
Ezekiel 44:28-30	Proverbs 21:20, LB Proverbs 30:24-25
Genesis 15:2-4	
Genesis 24:35-36	Genesis 41:34-36
Genesis 25:5	Isaiah 48:17
Genesis 31:14-16	Ecclesiastes 11:2

Proverbs 24:27
Matthew 8:14
Mark 1:29
Luke 4:38
Matthew 8:20
Acts 28:30
Ecclesiastes 5:13-14
Ecclesiastes 5:13-16, LB Proverbs 21:5
Proverbs 21:5, LB Proverbs 21:5
Proverbs 28:20
Proverbs 28:22
Ecclesiastes 3:1
Proverbs 27:23-27
Luke 14:28-29
Proverbs 20:18
Proverbs 21:5
Proverbs 24:3-4, LB
1 Corinthians 14:40
1 Corinthians 14:33
Jeremiah 9:23-24
1 Timothy 6:17
James 1:9-11
Jeremiah 48:7
Jeremiah 49:4-5
1 Timothy 6:17
1 Timothy 6:18
Isaiah 5:8

Leviticus 25:14-17
Proverbs 20:14
Proverbs 31:10, 16, 24
Deuteronomy 15:7-9
Psalm 112:5
Matthew 5:42
Exodus 22:25
Leviticus 25:35-37
Deuteronomy 23:19
Nehemiah 5:3-12
Deuteronomy 23:20
Psalm 15:1, 5
Ezekiel 18:7-17
Proverbs 28:8
Ezekiel 18:10, 13
Ezekiel 22:12-13
Habakkuk 2:6-7
Deuteronomy 23:20
Exodus 22:26-27
Deuteronomy 24:6, 10-13
Deuteronomy 24:17
Job 22:5-6
Ezekiel 18:7, 9, 16-17
Ezekiel 33:15
Ezekiel 18:10, 12-13
Amos 2:6, 8
Job 24:3, 9
Luke 6:34-35

CHILDREN

Deuteronomy 4:9
Deuteronomy 6:6-7

Deuteronomy 11:18-19
Proverbs 22:6

BUDGETING

Proverbs 27:23-27
Luke 14:28-29
1 Corinthians 14:40
1 Corinthians 14:33

Proverbs 20:18
Proverbs 21:5
Proverbs 24:3-4

CONTENTMENT

Philippians 4:11-13
Matthew 6:25-34
Luke 12:22-31
Hebrews 13:5-6
1 Timothy 6:8

Luke 3:14
Psalm 73:25
1 Timothy 6:6
Proverbs 6:35

COVETING

Exodus 20:17
Deuteronomy 5:21
Deuteronomy 7:25
Joshua 6:18
Micah 2:1-3
Joshua 7:11-25
1 Corinthians 10:6

1 Corinthians 6:9-10
Ephesians 5:3, 5
1 Corinthians 5:9-11
Acts 20:33
Exodus 34:23-24
Romans 7:7-8

EVIL USES OF MONEY

Matthew 26:14-15
Matthew 27:3-10
Mark 14:10-11
Luke 22:3-5
Acts 1:18
Genesis 37:28
Numbers 22:7

Numbers 22:18
Numbers 24:13
Esther 3:9-11
Esther 4:7
Judges 16:4-5
Judges 16:18
Judges 9:4

GREED

Ephesians 5:3, 5
Colossians 3:5
Luke 12:15
Proverbs 23:1-3
Psalm 73:25
1 Thessalonians 2:5
1 Corinthians 10:6
Numbers 11:4-5
1 Samuel 14:32
Isaiah 56:11
Romans 1:28-29
Psalm 10:3-4

Proverbs 11:6
2 Peter 2:1-3
2 Peter 2:14-15
Proverbs 30:15
Ezekiel 23:29-30
Micah 1:7
Ezekiel 33:31
Numbers 11:34
2 Kings 5:20-27
Jeremiah 6:12-13
Jeremiah 8:10

IDOLATRY

Exodus 20:23
Psalm 135:15
Hosea 1:8, 13
Colossians 3:5

Ezekiel 23:29-30
Micah 1:7
Isaiah 30:22-23
Judges 17:2-4

PARTIALITY

Deuteronomy 10:17, 2
Chronicles 19:7
Job 34:19
Ephesians 6:9
Proverbs 28:21
James 2:8-9
James 2:1-9
Exodus 23:3

Leviticus 19:15
Deuteronomy 1:17
Deuteronomy 16:18-19
2 Chronicles 19:6-7
Malachi 2:9
Romans 12:16
Philippians 2:3

TAXES/TRIBUTE

Romans 13:5-7
Matthew 22:17-21
Mark 12:14-17
Luke 20:22-25
2 Kings 3:4
2 Kings 15:20
2 Kings 23:33, 35
Ezra 6:8
1 Samuel 17:25
Ezra 7:24

Matthew 17:24-27
1 Kings 4:21
2 Kings 17:1-3
2 Chronicles 17:5
2 Chronicles 17:12
2 Chronicles 27:5
2 Chronicles 36:3
Ezra 4:20
Ezra 4:13

POOR

Exodus 22:21-24
Job 34:28
Proverbs 28:3
Isaiah 32:6-7
Proverbs 28:15
Proverbs 30:14
Job 20:10, 15, 18-20, 26, 28
Psalm 37:14-15
Psalm 109:11, 16
Proverbs 22:16
Proverbs 22:22-23
Isaiah 3:14-15
Isaiah 10:1-2
Jeremiah 22:1-5
Ezekiel 22:7, 29
Amos 2:6-7
Amos 4:1-2
Amos 5:9-12
Amos 8:4-6
Zechariah 7:9-12
Malachi 3:5

Psalm 94:2, 6, 7
Jeremiah 2:34
Mark 12:38-40
Luke 20:46-47
Ecclesiastes 5:8
Proverbs 31:8-9
Isaiah 1:17
Jeremiah 21:12
Proverbs 29:7
Job 30:25
Psalm 41:1-3
Proverbs 19:17
Proverbs 29:14
Jeremiah 7:5-9
Luke 14:12-23
Exodus 23:6
Deuteronomy 24:17
Daniel 4:25-27
Jeremiah 5:27-29
Ezekiel 16:49
Isaiah 1:23

Proverbs 14:31
Proverbs 17:5
Deuteronomy 10:18
Job 5:15
Psalm 9:18
Psalm 10:14
Psalm 12:5
Psalm 34:6
Psalm 35:10
Psalm 40:17
Psalm 68:6
Psalm 68:10
Psalm 69:33
Psalm 102:17
Psalm 107:4
Psalm 109:31
Psalm 113:7
Psalm 132:15
Psalm 140:12
Psalm 146:7
Psalm 146:9
Psalm 147:6
Proverbs 15:25
Isaiah 11:4
Isaiah 14:30
Isaiah 25:4
Isaiah 41:17
Jeremiah 20:13
Psalm 72:4, 10, 12-15
Psalm 74:21
Psalm 82:3-4
Psalm 109:21-22
Job 24:2-12, 14
Revelation 2:9
Revelation 3:17-18
1 Corinthians 1:26-27
Proverbs 22:2

Proverbs 29:13
Ecclesiastes 6:8
Proverbs 14:20
Proverbs 19:4
Proverbs 19:7
Proverbs 13:23
Proverbs 18:23
Proverbs 22:7
Ecclesiastes 9:14-16
Proverbs 10:15
Proverbs 30:7-9
Luke 6:20, 24
James 2:5
Isaiah 61:1
Matthew 11:2-5
Luke 4:18
Luke 7:22
Proverbs 13:8
Luke 16:19-25
James 1:9-10
Isaiah 29:19
Proverbs 28:11
Proverbs 19:1
Proverbs 19:22
Proverbs 28:6
1 Samuel 18:23
Psalm 70:5
Psalm 86:1
Lamentations 1:11
Luke 2:22-24
1 Corinthians 4:11-12
2 Corinthians 6:4-5, 10
2 Corinthians 11:27
Philippians 4:11-14
1 Corinthians 11:18-22
Leviticus 25:11-13
Leviticus 25:39-54

Jeremiah 34:13-17
Proverbs 13:18
Proverbs 20:13
Proverbs 21:17
Proverbs 23:20-21
Deuteronomy 15:4-5
2 Kings 24:14

2 Kings 25:12
Jeremiah 39:10
Jeremiah 40:7
Jeremiah 52:15
OTHER AREAS ADDRESSING
POOR: Lending, Partiality, Work

RICHES

Revelation 2:9
Job 5:5
Job 15:29
Job 20:10, 15, 18-20, 26, 28
Job 21:13, 16
Job 22:23-25
Job 27:13, 16-17
Job 36:11
Job 36:19
Ecclesiastes 7:11-12
Psalm 49:16-20
Ecclesiastes 5:13-15
1 Timothy 6:7
Psalm 39:6
Psalm 49:5-8
Proverbs 11:4
Matthew 16:26
Mark 8:36-37
Luke 9:25
Proverbs 14:20
Proverbs 19:4
Proverbs 23:4-5
Hebrews 11:24-26
1 Peter 1:7
1 Peter 1:18
Philippians 3:7-8

1 Timothy 6:17
Ecclesiastes 2:4-11
Job 28:15-19
Psalm 37:16
Psalm 119:14
Psalm 119:72
Psalm 119:127
Proverbs 3:13-16
Proverbs 8:10-11
Proverbs 8:18-21
Proverbs 15:16
Proverbs 16:8
Proverbs 16:16
Proverbs 16:19
Proverbs 19:1
Proverbs 20:15
Proverbs 22:1
Proverbs 28:6
Luke 12:48
Proverbs 13:21
Proverbs 15:6
Psalm 1:1-3
Psalm 22:29
Psalm 106:5
Psalm 122:6-7
Psalm 128:5

3 John 2

Genesis 12:5

Genesis 13:2

Genesis 15:13-14

Genesis 24:1

Genesis 24:16

Genesis 24:35

Genesis 26:12-14

Genesis 30:43

Genesis 33:11

Genesis 41:42

Genesis 45:13

Genesis 46:6

Genesis 47:27

Joshua 22:8

Ruth 2:1

2 Samuel 1:24

1 Kings 10:4, 7

1 Kings 3:11-13

1 Chronicles 29:23

1 Chronicles 29:28

2 Chronicles 1:11-12

2 Chronicles 9:22

2 Chronicles 17:5

2 Chronicles 17:11-12

2 Chronicles 18:1

2 Chronicles 32:27-30

Nehemiah 9:25

Job 1:3

Daniel 3:30

Matthew 27:57

1 Corinthians 4:8, 11-12

Philippians 4:11-18

Psalm 35:27

Hebrews 11:36-40

Revelation 5:12

Proverbs 14:24

Proverbs 24:3-4

Proverbs 21:17

Proverbs 22:16

Psalm 62:10

Ezekiel 28:4-5

1 Timothy 6:17

James 1:9-11

Jeremiah 9:23-24

Proverbs 10:15

Proverbs 18:11

Psalm 30:6-7

Psalm 49:10-12

Genesis 13:5-11

Genesis 26:12-16

Genesis 36:6-7

Isaiah 5:8

1 Corinthians 11:18-22

Proverbs 11:18

Matthew 13:4-5, 7, 22

Mark 4:2-3, 7, 18-19

Luke 8:7, 14

Matthew 19:16-26

Mark 10:17-27

Luke 18:28-30

Luke 16:19-25

Proverbs 28:11

Proverbs 18:23

Proverbs 22:7

James 2:6-7

Deuteronomy 6:10-12

Deuteronomy 8:9-18

Deuteronomy 31:20

Proverbs 30:7-9

Jeremiah 22:21-22

Revelation 3:17-18

Genesis 26:12-14, 16

Genesis 31:1

Proverbs 13:8
Ecclesiastes 5:12
Luke 6:24
James 5:1-5
Psalm 10:3-5
Psalm 37:1-2, 7, 9-11
Psalm 73:1-20
Proverbs 11:16
Jeremiah 12:1-2
1 Samuel 25:2
Esther 1:4
Esther 5:11
Isaiah 2:7
Ezekiel 27:33
Daniel 11:2
Luke 19:2
Deuteronomy 23:6
Ezra 9:12
Hosea 12:8
Zechariah 11:5
Judges 17:13
Proverbs 2:4
Ecclesiastes 10:20
Proverbs 13:7
Matthew 13:44-46
Proverbs 10:20

Isaiah 15:7
Jeremiah 51:13
Ezekiel 27:3, 12-27
Hosea 10:1-2
Zephaniah 1:11, 13, 18
Zechariah 9:3-4
Deuteronomy 17:16-17
1 Kings 4:26
1 Kings 10:14-28
2 Chronicles 1:14-17
2 Chronicles 9:8-27
Psalm 45:12
Isaiah 39:2, 4-6
Isaiah 60:5-6, 9, 11
Isaiah 61:6-7
Haggai 2:7
Zechariah 1:17
Zechariah 7:7
Revelation 6:15-16
Revelation 13:16-17
Revelation 17:4
Revelation 18:3
Revelation 18:11-19
Genesis 34:10-12
Genesis 34:21, 23
1 Samuel 17:25

MISCELLANEOUS

1 Kings 10:29
Proverbs 20:14
James 4:13-15
Proverbs 5:10
Proverbs 6:35
Proverbs 29:3
Proverbs 23:6-8

Ezekiel 33:31
James 3:14-16
James 4:2-3
2 Peter 2:3
Deuteronomy 21:14
Isaiah 13:17
2 Samuel 21:4

Ruth 3:10	Obadiah 1:13
Proverbs 11:26	Obadiah 1:6, 11
Proverbs 12:9	Micah 4:13
Proverbs 23:23	Nahum 2:9-10
Isaiah 53:9	Nahum 3:1
Matthew 13:52	Habakkuk 2:6-8
Mark 5:25-26	Zephaniah 1:11, 13, 18
Acts 22:28	Zephaniah 2:9
Proverbs 17:26	2 Corinthians 8:13-15
Isaiah 7:23	1 Timothy 2:9
Isaiah 23:18	Exodus 21:18-19
Isaiah 52:13	Exodus 21:22
Isaiah 53:10	Exodus 21:28-30
Isaiah 55:1-2	Exodus 21:32-36
Ezekiel 16:33-34	1 Samuel 8:10-11, 14-17
Ezekiel 48:14	Ezekiel 45:7-8,
Zechariah 11:12-13	Jeremiah 32:6-7, 9, 14-15
Mark 4:24-25	Jeremiah 32:25
Luke 15:8-10	Ezekiel 7:11-13, 19
Acts 2:44-45	Ezekiel 38:10-13
Acts 4:32-37	Daniel 11:24
Acts 19:18-19	Daniel 11:38
Genesis 20:16	Daniel 11:43
Genesis 34:27-29	Zechariah 14:1-2
1 Samuel 17:53	Zechariah 14:14
1 Kings 20:1-6, 8	Luke 17:28
2 Kings 14:12, 14	2 Timothy 3:1-2
2 Chronicles 20:25	Revelation 6:6
Ezra 9:7	Revelation 6:15-16
Esther 8:11	Revelation 9:20-21
Esther 9:5, 10	Revelation 13:16-17
Isaiah 10:5-6	Revelation 17:4
Isaiah 10:12-14	Revelation 18:3
Ezekiel 26:12	Revelation 18:11-19
Ezekiel 30:4	Jeremiah 7:5-9, 11
Hosea 13:15	Micah 3:11
Amos 3:11	Matthew 21:12-13